PRAISE FOR *KINGMAKER*

"Cini's game is strong: high energy, high personal values, a focus and passion for her work. If your career is worth saving or worth upgrading, then Cini's book is a *must read*. Written with candor and knowledge, *Kingmaker* is a blueprint on what to expect and how to achieve in a fast-paced environment without losing yourself."

Frank Novak
Special Teams Consultant, Green Bay Packers

"I intend to buy this book for each of our staff members. It's a clear, concise guide on how employees can achieve excellence, contribute to corporate goals, AND satisfy their personal and professional objectives. In this insightful book. Ms. Cini tells you how to demand more of yourself, your company, and your managers and come out a winner."

Christine Watkins
President and CEO, INVISION Inc.

"Finally, a mentor for each of us. This is a wonderful guided tour of life in corporate America, written in complete, sometimes painful, honesty. Joanne [Cini] is a career counselor without an agenda or conflict of interest. She gives the reader an up close and personal look at the work world, while insisting on a close and honest look in the mirror. Ultimately, *Kingmaker* is a very personal journey on the road to self-reliance and personal responsibility."

Lisa G. Churchville, President and General Manager
WJAR-TV in Providence, Rhode Island

"*Kingmaker* is a new twist on an old adage: to thine own self be true. Cini's contention, that you must take control of your own life and career in order to define your value potential in the competitive market of big business, is an important lesson for anyone looking to succeed in today's business world."

Ray Heacox
CEO, MediaOcean, a DDS Company

"For most of us, empowerment is still a buzz word. Cini, like the mentor you always wanted, guides you to its full meaning in your career—to purposeful, wide-eyed analysis and decisions about what's right for you."

Wendy Tynan
General Manager, Rogen International

"The journey Joanne takes us through is based on her own personal odyssey. That said, anyone who has spent a day in the life of Corporate America will relate to her observations. This is an astute chronicle of pitfalls to avoid, road bumps to maneuver, and challenges to aspire to. ENJOY THE RIDE!"

Bill Cella
Chairman, MAGNA Global USA

"Honesty is pure oxygen in a world dominated by cynics. Joanne Cini's efforts to instruct others based on her experiences—honest lessons learned in one of the world's pressure cookers, New York City broadcasting—is worth taking note of."

Louis Columbus
Senior Analyst, AMR Research

"Joanne has used her extensive business world experiences to put together a very informative primer for those involved in today's workforce. A necessary read."

Dennis Swanson
EVP and COO, Viacom Television Stations Group

Kingmaker

BE THE ONE YOUR COMPANY WANTS TO KEEP . . .

ON *YOUR* TERMS

Joanne Cini

PRENTICE HALL
An Imprint of PEARSON EDUCATION
Upper Saddle River, NJ • New York • London • San Francisco • Toronto • Sydney
Tokyo • Singapore • Hong Kong • Cape Town • Madrid
Paris • Milan • Munich • Amsterdam

www.ft-ph.com

Library of Congress Cataloging-in-Publication Data

Cini, Joanne.
  Kingmaker : be the one your company wants to keep-- on your terms / Joanne Cini.
    p. cm.
  ISBN 0-13-184030-4 -- ISBN 0-13-009025-5
    1. Career development. 2. Success in business. 3. Office politics. I. Title: Kingmaker.
  II. Title.

HF5381.C6565 2004

2003062415

Production Editor and Compositor: *Vanessa Moore*
VP, Executive Editor: *Tim Moore*
Development Editor: *Russ Hall*
Full-Service Production Manager: *Anne R. Garcia*
Marketing Manager: *John Pierce*
Manufacturing Buyer: *Maura Zaldivar*
Manfacturing Manager: *John Pierce*
Cover Design Director: *Jerry Votta*
Cover Design: *Mary Jo DeFranco*
Interior Design: *Gail Cocker-Bogusz*

 © 2004 Joanne Cini
Published by Pearson Education, Inc.
Publishing as Prentice Hall
Upper Saddle River, NJ 07458

Prentice Hall offers excellent discounts on this book when ordered in quantity for bulk purchases or special sales. For more information, please contact: U.S. Corporate and Government Sales, 1-800-382-3419, corpsales@pearsontechgroup.com. For sales outside of the U.S., please contact: International Sales, 1-317-581-3793, international@pearsontechgroup.com.

Printed in the United States of America
1st Printing

ISBN 0-13-184030-4

Pearson Education Ltd.
Pearson Education Australia Pty., Limited
Pearson Education Singapore, Pte. Ltd.
Pearson Education North Asia Ltd.
Pearson Education Canada, Ltd.
Pearson Educación de Mexico, S.A. de C.V.
Pearson Education—Japan
Pearson Education Malaysia, Pte. Ltd.

To my parents, Philip and Rita Cini

Mom and Dad, this book is in honor of your dedication to our family and the great examples you gave to Nancy, Suzanne, Phil, and me. Your values are alive in us. Thank you so much for all of your life lessons, unwavering support, and consistent love.

CONTENTS

Acknowledgments   IX

Introduction   XI

Part I People, Profit, Politics, and Process   1

Chapter 1   Who's a Kingmaker?   3
Chapter 2   The Seismic Shift   9
Chapter 3   A Word about Profit   21
Chapter 4   Politics at Large   27
Chapter 5   Politics in the Day to Day   35
Chapter 6   Losing Like a Winner   47
Chapter 7   Ego, Fear, and Competition   57
Chapter 8   The Responsibility of Leadership   67
Chapter 9   The Champion   75
Chapter 10   Embrace Diversity   81

Summary of Part I   People, Profit, Politics,
                    and Process   89

Part II Excel, Execute, Enjoy!   91

Chapter 11   Value Yourself If
             You Intend to Be Valuable   93
Chapter 12   How Can You Affect
             the Company's Margin?   103

CHAPTER 13   BECOME YOUR MANAGER'S
             GO-TO PERSON   111

CHAPTER 14   GETTING A HANDLE ON
             OBSESSION AND DEFENSIVE ACTION   117

CHAPTER 15   WHEN IS IT OKAY TO BREAK RANK?   129

CHAPTER 16   INTERVIEW DISCOVERY   137

CHAPTER 17   HOW TO PICK (AND GET
             ALONG WITH) YOUR BOSS   145

CHAPTER 18   MANAGEMENT BY TYPE   153

CHAPTER 19   PREPARING FOR YOUR ANNUAL REVIEW:
             MANAGING YOUR VALUE PERCEPTION   167

CHAPTER 20   KEEPING CLEAR ON WHAT
             YOU THINK YOU WANT   175

SUMMARY OF PART II   EXCEL, EXECUTE, ENJOY!   181

PART III   PLANNING FOR PASSION AND PROSPERITY   185

CHAPTER 21   BRANDING YOURSELF:
             THE ART OF FREE AGENCY   187

CHAPTER 22   ACHIEVING FULFILLMENT
             THROUGH GREAT WORK   199

CHAPTER 23   LETTING GO AND HAVING A LIFE   207

CHAPTER 24   THE FREEDOM PLAN   213

CHAPTER 25   WHEN LEAVING IS THE ONLY ANSWER   231

SUMMARY OF PART III   PLANNING FOR PASSION
                      AND PROSPERITY   237

CHAPTER 26   YOUR PERSONAL VALUE KINGDOM   241

Acknowledgments

To my sisters and brother, Nancy, Suzanne and Phil: Thank you so much for your support, love, laughter, and truth. Thanks for your time and sincere encouragement that is never a question. I love you.

A hearty thanks goes to my very personal board of directors—my dear and great friends. I am a blessed and lucky woman to have you in my life. Thank you for your friendship always, but especially in the year I was deciding to change my life. Your support, patience, kindness, insight, and advice helped me a great deal. Your generosity of spirit, experience and courage are alive in these pages. Also, in loving memory and in the exuberant spirit of my dear friend Lynne Thigpen.

To my closest non-sister sister, Janet Riccio. Janet, words cannot describe the depths of my thanks to you. Your intervention when I was lonely and low taught me a most valuable life lesson that I will carry for the rest of my life: People who love you want to help you, just ask. You challenged me to speak my whole truth to you so that I could finally hear myself. Spaghetti vongole will never be the same again.

A huge thanks goes to my agent, Rob Wilson. Rob, thank you for taking me on as a first-time author. Your guidance and belief in my work validated the efforts and kept me going. Your support and diligence made this happen.

I could not have been more fortunate than to be associated with Prentice Hall, especially as my first experience as an author. Every person I worked with was upbeat, honest, generous, willing and professional. Special salute to Executive Editor Tim Moore for amassing a great team and for granting my contract for *Kingmaker*. Thank you, thank you, thank you! May there be more.

The intimacy and vulnerability involved in sharing your voice with a stranger is a daunting and intimidating experience. Development Editor Russ Hall is one tough Texan and we worked each other hard. Russ, you were spot-on with your suggestions and you probably didn't bargain on being my teacher and mentor, too. Your work made every bit of difference in this book. I'll never look at a pronoun, a split infinitive, or a fishing rod the same way again.

Louis Columbus, Cleo Coy, and Teresa Horton helped to keep the book on message, on key, and in full comma. Thanks to Mary Jo DeFranco for the cover and Vanessa Moore for your kind and skilled handling of the format, look and feel of the book. You two gave this book its face.

To all of the great bosses I've had: Thank you for challenging your workforce while caring about the integrity of the environment. A special thanks goes to Ray Heacox for the collaboration that was the highlight of my career. To all of my not-so-great bosses, thank you for making me stronger. You will see more of yourselves in Chapter 18.

To all of my wonderful former colleagues who continue to be my friends: Thank you for your alliance, support, challenge, learning and kindness through the years and for your insights that appear in this book. To those who chose competition over collaboration and ego over confidence: There is still hope.

I hope you will enjoy this book.

INTRODUCTION: You're Outta Here Kid!

Dateline: Christmas 2000, my office at a major TV network-owned stations division, New York, New York . . .

It was 2 P.M. on the first day back from a much needed holiday break. My head was already filled with the rolling familiar tapes of poisonous, negative-speak. I was falling fast back into depression and hate mode and with a consistent, demonic cadence, my mind repeated over and over and over again, "I hate this place, I hate these people, I hate my life."

I am normally an optimistic and happy woman who believes wasting a day in negativity to be the greatest sin of all. Hell, I hate hate. The truth is that I'd been living in a sea of job-related sadness for most of 2000 and I could not spend one more day feeling this way. Misery was permeating my whole life and pushing me out of my career.

A visit with my family in Michigan over the Christmas holiday helped to put me in a very mellow state. I'd originally returned to my workplace on Wednesday, in the middle of the workweek, but I found that I could not bring myself to open e-mail. I couldn't bear to see the 200-or-so messages waiting for me, many marked urgent with text raging in capital letters. I moved to hit the button a few times, but my finger refused to go there.

I called a close friend to meet me for lunch. Debbie and I had a dose of great friendship at The Post House and after a pleasant time I went back to my pen. I stared at the computer again and decided, instead, to go to a movie—a comedy or romance—and not return to work until the following Tuesday, the day after New Year's.

I was a vice president at a standout company and by anyone's standards, on top of my game. Resilience and a positive mental attitude helped to steer me through 24 years in television, culminating in management and executive roles at the TV stations divisions of the four major networks. My career traversed from first female sales manager at an ABC-owned TV station, to vice president of local sales at Rupert Murdoch's FOX, to Six Sigma greenbelt and high-potential senior vice president at Jack Welch's GE/NBC. I was instrumental in three startups, including the sales and marketing of a new network, a national rep firm, and a network-television-owned stations Internet group. I hired and managed hundreds of people, supervised nearly two billion dollars in revenue, helped to create winning environments, and managed change. I mostly had a great time for those 24 years until the rose-colored glasses broke.

I was on board with FOX at its beginning and helped to launch *A Current Affair.* We had the daring to go against Katie Couric and Bryant Gumbel with *Good Day New York.* We positioned the new FOX network to the New York marketplace with shows like *Melrose Place, Beverly Hills 90210,* and *The Simpsons.* I was at WCBS when David Letterman came on board and CBS tried to turn its prime-time boat around with *Chicago Hope* and *Central Park West.* I worked at NBC during the real "Must See TV" days and was proud to position *The West Wing* and *The Golden Globes* to our customers.

I was part of excellent, exclusive training classes and complex negotiations and creative strategy sessions. I traveled across the country and met interesting people while we entertained at the best places. I was one of three people to open and operate—from scratch—an in-house representation firm for a network-television-owned stations group with a body of 150 people in 13 offices nationwide. We built nirvana and kept it for three years, before agendas changed, and the business changed, and the world changed.

I had a smile on my face for most of two decades. I led successful charges, hired and helped to promote many people, started an associates program targeted toward diversity, and created healthy, thriving environments built to win with as little conflict as possible. I laughed out loud, danced at parties, celebrated mighty successes, and always bellowed a song, impromptu, as I walked the halls of whichever place I worked in at the time.

I was always wide-eyed and idealistic and oh so hopeful. Without realizing it, I became a free agent early on. I'd join a company full of vigor and energy and give all I had to make it a better place. I see now that there was always an arc: a new, exciting, challenging learning curve, followed by lots of hard work, team building, strategizing, and the win. Ultimately there would be some ownership change, or management change, or agenda change that transposed everything, soured the place, and propelled a move. I always loved the work. I always hated selfish, egomaniacal, unkind, blustery, political behavior and the toxic air that it spread. I fought through sexual harassment and unequal pay and boys clubs and exclusive, cliquey, cancerous groups. The higher I went, the higher the stakes and the harder and more expensive the game.

I just kept working and beating odds and doing it my way, in sync with my core personal and business values. I'd just go to the next place when the beauty ran out. I see now that I had worked at four different places because I believed it was possible to find joy and soul in my work, even in a corporate environment, even for a while. I believed we could make great TV, serve and inform the public, improve people's lives, and still make money. I worked and worked and would eventually hit a wall and go to the next place when the environment, the learning curve, or the political climate changed to my displeasure. I was a searcher—always an optimistic believer that we could deliver great business with integrity, dignity, honesty, and teamwork, and the details such as money, promotion, and attribution would follow, because they were supposed to. And they did, enough to keep me going.

I mostly had a great time. I worked hard, made some great friends, had very successful results, displayed mental toughness, took care of my reputation, and protected my character.

All I ever wanted was a healthy environment and the opportunity for great work, and I had it in many situations over the years. However, the constantly dramatic shifts in culture, politics, leadership, and attitude, and blind eyes to bad behavior, began to force a double personality upon me, with worker on one side and internal political strategist on the other. The split was making me sick; it was sort of like being a Democrat and having to live and act and work like a Republican.

> *The split was making me sick; it was sort of like being a Democrat and having to live and act and work like a Republican.*

I did it mostly my way for 24 years and, mostly, it worked. I was 47 years old and on top of my game and, in the end, I was absolutely miserable.

I was alarmed on my return from that satisfying holiday break that it had taken only a few hours for my head to return to the hate reel. I realized that not one time in the 10 beautiful days spent in my personal world had I thought those ugly words. Not once—and that was probably the greatest relief and most insightful quiet of all.

I went home from work that night and said to myself, "This is it kid, you're outta there." I looked at a calendar. It was January 2, 2001; May 18 became my initial target date. I would give notice in early April. In the meantime, I would continue to work hard, keep my eyes on the freedom prize, and save every possible dime. I'd left jobs and companies before, but this was different. This time I was leaving my career to start a new life that was not clearly defined in my mind's eye.

Of course, I didn't just wake up one day and say, "I'm going to quit my job and leave my career." Not after investing nearly half of my life in it. I was employed by one of the best companies in the world, and I had achieved a high level, earning very high pay, with great perks and a repertoire of experiences that spanned Super Bowls, Olympic Games, Final Fours, and U.S. Open tennis and golf. I went to the Emmys and the Grammys and the Tony Awards. I also knew that I really didn't hate these people; it was just my own dramatic hyperbole and I couldn't turn it off. The hate recordings in my mind were starting to affect my soul.

I'd always taken care of my money to have the freedom to make a career change or retire early, but could I really do it? Leaving my company and my corporate career was a most serious matter that took the better part of a year to resolve. I took the planning and strategic lessons I'd learned in the workplace and began applying them to my own life in preparation of my leave. I came to understand the game had changed, or maybe I had. I looked around my company and the industry and decided that there wasn't a different job that I wanted; I wanted out. The rate of return on my investment was now in the deficit column and this was the scariest unfolding, as it required the biggest self-directed change of my life. As challenging and difficult as the work life could be, it also supplied great learning, stimulation, security, excitement, routine, status, and social contacts.

I anticipated every possible crisis after the break and prepared personal toolkits to have on hand in case I came to regret my decision on any level. I waited until the time was right by continuing to work hard while I prepared mentally and emotionally. I knew the time was right when my finger would not hit the e-mail button. I was done. I could no longer be the worker bee making yet another king, deserving or not. In the end, I left my television career on March 31, 2001. Since then, I have looked back only to learn from my past.

The first order of business after leaving was a total career review. I wrote a memoir that forced an honest look back at each of the four broadcast companies I'd worked for to identify growth and challenges and to study the significant events and the people that affected my life. I was looking for the reasons I stayed so long and for the truths that gave me license to leave this place, this industry that I loved and was part of. I reviewed my career and rediscovered the areas of true passion, fulfillment, and joy that kept me thriving. The memoir also highlighted the recurring political themes that always propelled a move. Writing the memoir was the first step in my healing process and the first ingredient of a successful transition to my new life.

The career review was as illuminating as a bolt of lightning on a dark night. Many memories brought great happiness in the retelling and found me reliving the excitement and fulfillment, recalling the pride and joys, and remembering all of the reasons I loved my work. Some of the writing proved so painful I had to leave the project for days at a time. I was left feeling spent all over again with the added ingredients of sadness and an impulse to heal this person of the past. I was amazed that so much had happened in one career lifetime and that I was able to move and thrive through it. It had all passed so quickly and I am richer in every way for the experience.

The memoir proved educational as well. Maturity, rest, self-truth, and calm have given me a new set of eyes. Time and distance have given me a wealth of insight that came from the very center of the person that I am and always was. I saw the things I did right, the things I wish someone had mentored me more about, and the things I wish I'd listened to or understood better.

The immediate question became what to do with this new knowledge from my most personal place that will surely be revisited by many, especially now with corporate conduct and career security in such turmoil. There is surely a way to remain yourself, hold on to your dreams, and stay true to your long-term life goals while you navigate the rigorous career path in front of you.

> *There is surely a way to remain yourself, hold on to your dreams, and stay true to your long-term life goals while you navigate the rigorous career path in front of you.*

I hope you will hear what I have to say and make your own decisions from questions that will be raised. Perhaps my insights and mistakes will lead you to think twice before making your own. I realize that everyone must find his or her own way, but I also know it helps to be conscious and aware. This book could serve as a flashlight in case you need a little light on your own road. Most of the views and observances are from my professional life that spanned 24 years of work, growth, and change over many highs and a few significant lows. I have also incorporated the views of many respected colleagues into the subjects of several chapters.

This book is a day-to-day career-thrive guide enveloped in an understanding of big-picture business with an eye toward a holistic life. The company's basic mission is indeed that "it's all about results." You can come to understand this reality and serve it while enhancing your whole life. You *can* be exuberant in your work and learning while you hold on to yourself and your dreams. You can still make a difference. You can contribute to the company and to your own growth and find wondrous fulfillment in the honor of great work. Your mission, if you accept it, is to understand the game of corporate life and become valuable to an organization and an industry within the house rules, while fortifying your own personal value kingdom.

A personal value kingdom is yours to shape and fill. It might begin with a balanced life that includes the emotional, mental, spiritual, and physical aspects of a full life. The financial dimension should also be considered because money grants freedom from stress and worry and gives you the ability to make unencumbered choices. Your working life steps on the balance of each of these core aspects every day. The environment in which you spend the biggest part of your waking life can help to fulfill or strip the equilibrium in your life. If your work is all consuming, you might not have the mental capacity left to think about things other than work, to feel emotions other than those related to work, and most important, to be a centered, balanced, and happy person. Overwhelming deadlines or political situations might cause extreme pressure, but you can find

> *Fortifying your personal value kingdom means understanding the real deal in business and choosing who gets your talent and energy.*

ways to maneuver them that will leave you feeling fulfilled and substantive, with energy to spare for the other parts of your life.

Fortifying your personal value kingdom means deciding what is necessary for your sense of a full and fulfilling life and making time and room for it. It means understanding the real deal in business and choosing who gets your talent and energy. It means choosing which battles are worth fighting and which conversations are worth obsessing over. Fortification will come from working smarter so that you have the time and energy for a balanced life. Knowing yourself and your long-term, whole-life goals, while working in an honorable way, will lead you to great accomplishments in and outside of your career. It can be done. You only have to be conscious and ever diligent.

Gauging your reactions to change and growth through self-awareness along the way is the key to a balanced and centered approach to your career. Understand what motivates you while you consider what motivates those above and around you. Be aware of what you are getting into, where and why you want to move up, and what your opportunity risks are. Know your personal core values and how you can impress your environment with those ideals. Knowing what you want and how you fit, or need to adapt, will inform your decisions as you move on in your career.

In the course of the book we discuss the purpose of business and consider ways to navigate office politics. What is true and responsible leadership? How can you affect the company profit margin from any position? How important is your immediate boss and what do you need to know about him or her? Where do you fit in the larger scheme? What can you do to make yourself valuable? How can you be the most effective manager? When is it best to stay under the radar screen? What is a kingmaker?

We consider the importance of energy, leadership, and teamwork in achieving a goal and the advantages of adopting a champion. We'll also take a look at the places that ego, competition, and fear take in business and the difference between idealists and realists.

You must have your own confidence and financial security so that you can decide for yourself which projects you want to go for, if you mind working 24/7 or not, or suffer a bully boss or not.

Chapter 24, "The Freedom Plan," is about money and your relationship with it. Financial planning is paramount if you want choices in your life. It is vital to have your own security so that you don't ever have to be afraid of a threatened headcount reduction, or ageism, sexism, or cronyism. You must have your own confidence and financial security so that you can decide for yourself which projects you want to go for, if you mind working 24/7 or not, or suffer a bully boss or not. With a freedom plan you can decide to change careers if the day comes when your core values and passions are at odds with your current work environment. In short, plan to not be stuck anywhere because of money. You will have the ultimate freedom of choice and the opportunity to execute great work for the pure passion and joy of it.

Whatever you do and wherever you go, invest yourself into it and remember, always, to enjoy yourself. Having fun on the job is rewarding *and* contagious.

KINGMAKER

I

PEOPLE, PROFIT, POLITICS, AND PROCESS

1 WHO'S A KINGMAKER?

Who or what is a kingmaker? You might remember this FedEx commercial that aired in the winter of 2001: A group of a dozen or so people is huddled around a conference room table. All the workers in the room are in open shirts and ties, but the person at the head of the table, the boss, is in a suit. We join the meeting as the manager says, "We've got to save money, people. Ideas."

One member of the group contributes the idea that they open an online account with FedEx and save 10 percent on Express shipping immediately. Silence follows for a few beats, then the fellow at the head of the table looks straight ahead and repeats the exact words in authoritative tone with emphatic hand gestures to match.

The group loudly concurs as the camera moves to the face of the worker who proposed the idea in the first place. Perplexed, he declares, "You just said what I just said only you did this," as he mimics his boss's hand motions.

The boss looks not at him, but straight ahead, and says, "No, I did this," as he repeats his hand motion. The group of sycophants proclaims, "Bingo. Got it. Great." The camera captures the contributor, who has a sour grimace on his face.

This is a perfect example: The perplexed guy is a kingmaker who doesn't yet realize his own power.

Anyone in corporate America up to the CEO level is a king-maker. Actually, even the CEO has to make kings of the company shareholders. This also holds true whether you are in education, a not-for-profit organization, film, real estate, small business, or any sort of work in which there is more than one person involved. Everyone reports to someone who reports to someone else, and we each have a stake, whether we realize it or not, in our boss's growth to king status. King status is achieved through popularity via leadership or politics, and through results, which ultimately lead to growth and profit for the division, the company, and the shareholders.

Your great work helps your manager reach his or her corporate and career goals, and as a result you are more likely to reach your own.

The awareness of the unspoken roles of kingmaker and profit contributor, subtly folded into our careers, is vitally important to our own success. Your great work helps your manager reach his or her corporate and career goals, and as a result you are more likely to reach your own. The issue is to become an *aware* kingmaker by creating and understanding your value to this person and to the company while remaining true to yourself. Your agenda is to become a vital contributor, leader, motivator, and innovative thinker in whatever post you hold at whatever level. Become known as a results-oriented person who gets things done well. It is smart to take every action to identify a well-connected king-in-waiting to work for who can ultimately become your champion. Ideally, you will learn a great deal from this person, who will ultimately advocate for you (becoming *your* kingmaker) along the way.

Some of my friends and colleagues had a hard time with the notion of the worker as kingmaker, feeling that it is a subservient role. The reality is that not everyone can be a king outright; there simply aren't enough positions, and nobody can lead alone. Every leader needs people to rely on to bring objectives to life. The kingmaker station can make you very valuable and it is not an inferior role, but an important one. You know that you want to stretch in your career because you love challenge, change, and growth. You already understand that your job is to do your part to reach company objectives.

You can move up in the organization and feel very strong about your own security when at least two things happen with regularity.

First, competency is the baseline and excellence is the goal. For the record, competency means "average" in many companies today. On a performance appraisal-rating scale of 1 to 5, a competent label will yield a 3 rating. Who wants to be an average 3? Being competent is not enough to ensure security in a wobbly economy and tough job market. Because your work will speak for you, be conscious of the message you want to send with consistency. Second, it is imperative that you are recognized as a person who makes things happen, who is comfortable to be around, and who is ultimately trustworthy. When you are seen this way, the powers that be will want you on their team because it ensures their success. You will help them reach the company objectives and, as a result, their own personal career goals; the great news is that you will also be part of the team that makes things happen. You will grow to be your boss's probable successor, which is a necessary identification to make for either of you to be promoted. It is not subservient to be a kingmaker. It is a reality and it could be your ticket to becoming an insider with a strong career path in front of you.

Being a kingmaker is creating a trademark for yourself that is highly desirable to executives who have two goals: the company objectives and their own career growth.

Being a kingmaker does not mean being sycophantic or without original thought, vision, or personal motivation. Being a kingmaker is not even the same as managing up. It is creating a trademark for yourself that is highly desirable to executives who have two goals: the company objectives and their own career growth. How is this different from your own goals? You want to meet or exceed the company objectives and you want a great career track, too. Being a kingmaker also helps you identify the competencies of the people you'll want to hire to work for you so that you can be better prepared for the rise to king, if that is your goal.

Being a kingmaker means that you must excel in your day-to-day responsibilities while being aware of the overriding style and ambitions enveloped in the actions of the person to whom you report. The relationship between you and your manager is most fluent when your objectives and values are in sync. Achievement of your own goals is easier when you gain your king's support on the road to achievement.

Often personalities, politics, energy, and longevity in a position or place determine the kingmaker's success, measured in large part by his or her own sense of fulfillment and achievement gained on the job and in life overall. Being a kingmaker isn't always easy, especially if you don't have a great boss, if you get a new manager every six months, or if the prevailing mood is survival (fear) rather than moving forward (optimistic productivity). It can be especially difficult when you see your ideas credited to someone else, as in the previously mentioned FedEx commercial, and this happens with unfortunate frequency. The ethic of attribution does not apply the same way in business as it does in journalism, for example.

In my experience, it only felt bad to be a kingmaker when the king wasn't generous or inclusive, and when he or she was a narcissistic taker (or hoarder) of information, knowledge, and credit. There were many situations when I felt hidden or in the crossfire of territorial politics that I did not want to be a part of. So many egos with so little time! I should have done more to protect my position and contributions, and I see now that meant, in part, having a champion in a high place. It is more comfortable, credible, and efficient to have someone with clout advocate for you than to do it for yourself. The fact is that leaders get to present wins and losses the way they want to. The king gets the overall credit or blame for work in his or her department and attribution isn't always part of the leader's lexicon. You get paid to do a great job; a great boss is a real bonus.

> *It is more comfortable, credible, and efficient to have someone with clout advocate for you than to do it for yourself.*

The purpose of this book is to shine a light on this kingmaker role and to be a resource for your own career as you navigate your way in today's very tough work environment. I did very well, but maybe you can do even better.

Through the awareness of your role as kingmaker and profit contributor, you will excel in your work, your creativity and productivity will improve, you will be more secure, and you will enjoy a secret sense of purpose that does not have to conflict with your own core values. You will be free to be the best at what you do, become invaluable to your leader, and become one of the people that your company wants to keep and other companies want to steal away. You will thrive in your current organization with the confidence of a free agent who has the security of employment within your industry because of your strong work ethic and your good name.

It is up to you to take the driver's seat in your career and in your whole life, and the earlier the better.

2 THE SEISMIC SHIFT

Anxiety has always had its place in the work world. When everything is clicking you start each day in high spirits. You want to matter, learn, and grow in ways intellectual and financial and you want to enjoy yourself. Long-term goals are in place and some days you even see yourself in the driver's seat, running the whole show, with product or service, people, and profit all at the right pace and place. Irritants, such as unscheduled people, meetings, expectations, and quota changes, will regularly interrupt your path, but you'll move through it, because you can and you are pretty happy in your job and career overall.

Anxiety has upped the ante in this new day. Geopolitical turmoil, a sluggish economy, and technology are great drivers of change, but who would have believed that the very integrity of American business could be at stake because core values and standard earnings measurements had somehow been forgotten? We woke each day in the second half of 2002 wondering whose shoes would drop next in view of the recent turbulence: Enron, Global Crossing, Arthur Andersen, World-Com, Xerox, Tyco, and ImClone have led the way in activities no leader could be proud of. We watched as prominent business executives were hauled off under indictment for lying, stealing, and cheating. We watched as stocks lost 50 percent of their value in days because of *possible* associations with unethical conduct. Wal-Mart faced a class action lawsuit by low-wage workers who had been intimidated into working hours off the clock, and Wal-Mart is not alone in this activity. We are living and working in a day when government must intercede to ensure honesty. Beginning on August 14, 2002, CEOs have been asked to sign an affidavit swearing to the veracity of their profit and earning numbers.

Two million private sector jobs have been lost since 2001. Workers of all levels have been asked to take reduced bonuses or none at all, to expect no pay raise in the next year, and even to take pay cuts. If the choice is your job or a bad job market, you might have to take the cut quietly and die a little bit inside.

Two million private sector jobs have been lost since 2001.

You've probably wondered if your job will be next, if your 401(k) is at stake, if your options will be worth anything by the time you need them, and which of your leaders might bail out or need bail. You might worry about your own place in your industry and you might also be anxious about what mood your boss is in and what new crisis will flow downhill this day.

Andy Grove, chairman of Intel, was quoted in *The New York Times* on July 1, 2002: "The same way the market sentiment shifted toward an unbridled exuberance, the values of a lot of people managing companies in this market environment drifted toward 'me, me, me.' I've been in business for 40 years and I find myself feeling embarrassed and ashamed to be a businessman." Mr. Grove is not alone, and leaders whose very brand as an executive have been tarnished will undoubtedly come forward with new measures of accountability, whether legislated or not.

Who else feels this way? How about the people who put in an honest day and have no idea about maneuvers "upstairs" that might prove harmful to them? How about the investors who believe in the company's integrity and real growth? How are these people impacted, and what or who is helping them to cope?

We must discover which qualities in the corporate culture contributed to the recent malaise and which values still exist that can keep our workforce energized, enthused, and ready to execute. Morale and overall values are at risk when detrimental conduct is allowed and when profit and stock price are recognized as the company's primary driver.

Technological changes burst on the scene with one imprint being the increasing speed of information dissemination. E-mail, instant messaging, and electronic meetings are speeding up requests and pressure on the people that have to respond. Double tasking is now quadruple tasking, with fewer people to handle the load or even assist. The people left standing have no choice but to take on more work. More work at higher speed to meet tougher market demands creates a driving work experience. Add survival stress to this situation and you have political turmoil that can be worse than the workload. Leaders must be relentless drivers to see the work through to completion and achieve the desired results. People are on treadmills without control of the speed. The bean counters and head-counters have their hands on the speed dials now.

All of this madness boils down to probable imbalance for the already stressed employee. Do you feel it? To excel as opposed to just keeping up, you must become one-tracked, very organized, and focused like a horse in the Kentucky Derby, lest you dare feel what's happening to you. This leaves little time for a deep breath or thought. This speedball leaves little time for new ideas, family or friends, or other activities because it is so draining. Sometimes you just need to be completely quiet, on a couch, like a zombie. Or you continue on with a busy weekend life to stay connected to family, friends, and your own life, but you are preoccupied and not quite with them or it. And you are t-i-r-e-d.

The badge of honor to some is in the number of e-mails received, the number of hours worked, the number of business trips taken, and the number of vacations not taken. They complain with some perverse pride about the lunches grabbed and gobbled alone at their desk, the number of days they're away from their spouses and children, or the number of dates they don't have. Some people love this track and God love them because we need them to be happy.

This current badge of honor doesn't satisfy everyone, however. Maybe it's an age thing, a value thing, the aftermath of 9/11, or the corporate scandals, but people are beginning to take stock of their whole life and how job-related stress affects every area of it. The new value proposition that people are considering is how much of their life is worth spending on their work. Many of you are in it now and many of you have a thriving, fulfilling career in the face of any change because of the energy that you possess and because the culture and leadership that surrounds you is good and healthy. Good for you. Savor this.

A Thrash in Real Time

Through necessity I became almost completely work-focused for the last years of my career. I was the vice president of sales for an in-house TV stations group Internet startup, and part of a self-directed team. The leader of each segment—content, IT, strategy, sales, and process—were to work in concert although each of us reported separately to the president of the television stations division. We hit the ground running wildly, with no time or resources given to team building, a mission statement, or a cogent strategy from which to start. The team was dysfunctional to say the least. We were each on a treadmill, never in the same gym. We were disparate in our experiences, longevity, and expectations of team play. Rude behavior ruled the day. I had never been a part of anything like it. Have you ever been in a meeting where people have actually told others to shut up? I was in shock, I was embarrassed to be part of this "team," and I believed the whole thing was too petty to complain about to my boss. After all, he was the president of a division who oversaw several major-market television stations and the highest profit contribution to the overall company. He did acknowledge my dilemma one day by simply saying, "You are in a thrash." He knew. And I knew the chances were high that I would become collateral damage, a casualty of war.

The world of Internet advertising was being created as we worked it and our sales force were TV people. This meant a learning curve that included every bit of terminology, a new experience with inventory and "commercials," and a whole new set of advertising buyers, separate from the TV world. We had little in the way of appropriated money or people resources to handle the task and this meant my energy was spent traveling, teaching, and helping to create saleable convergent marketing programs. Some people in our sales force were resistant to the additional workload and saw little upside in becoming savvy in the next new thing. The energy was outgoing with little coming back for a good long time. I'd always had the great enjoyment of circular energy at work: feedback, brainstorming, and problem solving in tandem with a group (or at least one other person). I missed the positive interaction terribly and worked hard to create an ad-hoc community with the bright stars who grasped the new venture with enthusiasm and care. In time, these people became my lifeblood, but they were almost all in remote locations.

In the meantime, territory struggles developed because Internet revenue was viewed as the hot new growth opportunity, with lots of attention from the highest levels of the company, but the reality was that it represented a very small segment of overall revenue. Mixed messages from the television sales leadership ensued. With a wink of an eye they said, "Pay attention to this new effort, but don't dare to take your eye off the ball of our main revenue source, television." This was happening as that same leadership was trying to have Internet sales report to their area, meaning that I would be back where I started, no longer reporting to the president, but to the latest king-in-waiting. My job was made exponentially more difficult. I had to grab the attention of the sales constituency and infuse intelligence and excitement about the Web, over the mixed messages, while fighting off the cynics and the power hungry, who were one and the same.

This long-term one-way energy flow and political infighting was tiring and extremely isolating, and because this is not in sync with my normal balance and character, I was out of kilter and becoming increasingly unhappy. Survival mode forced the worst of me to compete with the best of me. I became more competitive and ego conscious to stay politically savvy and this drained energy I would rather have used elsewhere. I was simply tired of elbows in the face. I did not enjoy the political tussling and had no respect for the rude behavior that I witnessed over and over again. I found the workplace becoming less and less humane by the day, and the pressure of everyone's workload made it almost acceptable, or at least understandable. All of this negative energy took away from the joy of the work, not to mention the joy in my life. ∎

The road for many people is more treacherous now, and what was once a bastion for the unemotional can now be an emotional place. Intel's Andy Grove said he is "embarrassed." To walk around a company and witness a clipped pace, furrowed brow, arms flailing, and hands wringing is to see emotion in action. Celebrations and high-fives surrounded by cheers and laughter are the emotions you might enjoy more.

There is a way to hold on to yourself as you grow and learn and prosper in the face of more changes than you could ever imagine. Specifically, your part is to continue to work with integrity and to have the courage and internal relationships to call out behavior that you might witness that is not in line with the company culture or your own values. Your own day-to-day world will be served best by fearlessly embracing change as you manage your time and work processes to include new tasks, cut redundancies, and continue to be a positive, leading force in your area. Your internal value will grow when you understand the genesis of change and do your part to minimize fear, conflict and rumor, and through the consistent execution of excellent work.

> *There is a way to hold on to yourself as you grow and learn in the face of change. Your value will grow when you do your part to minimize fear, conflict and rumor, and through excellent work and results.*

The work world has changed and the power pendulum will swing again. What are the prospects for the future? How can you learn from the current environment to go beyond mere coping and navigation to fulfillment and success? Who will you let measure your success besides yourself? The power of your measure is yours to give; this is lesson number one. Repeat it often to yourself.

How do you move beyond the fear and survival mode that you might face in the perceived lack of long-term employment security? Workers in the 1950s through the 1980s often had an entire career at one company. The 1990s brought a new confidence and an entrepreneurial attitude fueled by the dot-com explosion. We witnessed company loyalty dwindle as employees made moves between corporations for more money, better perks, and swifter promotions, or to follow their king to the next new thing. The employer had to work harder to retain key employees; salaries grew.

The current bottom-line profit urgencies and a wealth of talented people in the unemployment lines have tilted the power in the job market toward the company. Corporate America is armed with Wall Street's acceptance of large head-count reductions. Today there is no dishonor in laying off a substantial percentage of the workforce; often the move is rewarded with a higher stock price. It is expensive to lay off a workforce or replace personnel in key positions. Streamlining is practical and smart; overcutting could expose a company to other risks such as mistakes, customer service problems, loss of creativity, and burnout, leading to the further bail out of important employees . . . each an expensive proposition in their own right.

New economic and technical retooling will force corporations to hire fewer but smarter workers. The sharp executive will want to staff his or her jobs with highly skilled, productive, long-term players. To thrive today, the employee must recognize this condition and move beyond the current survival and fear mode into a value and significance mode.

Today's lean corporations will hire fewer but smarter workers. To thrive today, you must recognize this condition and move beyond the current survival and fear mode into a value and significance mode.

There is a very wide silver lining in today's headcount economy. We could very well be headed for the ultimate meritocracy in which quality work will count for more and be rewarded. Companies will be leaner and, as such, each position must be filled with highly contributing personnel. People who deliver the competencies and the ultimate results will thrive. Cliques and cronyism might finally cease as the first road to success because a person in the king position will only afford the most productive and efficient, the highest potential people on his or her team. The onus to be recognized for your contributions is more important than ever, and the onus is largely on you to be understood as a key long-term player. *Four keys are consistent and imperative: excellent performance, truth, anticipation, and planning.*

Your immediate goal is to become an obvious value to the organization. Employees must now forge a way to incorporate the sensibilities of free agency while excelling in their current environment. There is a real second bottom line: You must be in the driver's seat when it comes to your career choices. Make the call on where you give your talent and spend so much of your life. Be the one your company wants to keep, and be the decision maker regarding where you stay. In the meantime, keep your underlying long-term dreams and passions alive while making your day-to-day life more enjoyable.

It is time to consider and create your own seismic shift in the ways that you view your career and your whole-life plan.

EXCEL ON THE JOB

Make it your business and your priority to become excellent in your workplace. Be valuable to an organization so that you will be the one who makes it through cuts in bad times. Understand the playing field, the leadership, the culture, and how you can enhance the place with your work and your values. Be in charge of your career and serve your responsibility to it. Focus, care, contribute endlessly and it will soon become effortless. It will just become who you are and it will inform your growth and your choices. Matter. Make the honor of your work bigger than your worst thoughts, fears, or nemesis. Thrive, excel, and grow. Use your work to make

> *Matter. Make the honor of your work bigger than your worst thoughts, fears, or nemesis. Use your work to make you smarter, better, happier, richer, and fuller.*

you smarter, better, happier, richer, and fuller. Make this as much of an objective as the work goal given to you by your manager. Get through the bad times by working harder and smarter and fight against letting the politics of the place ruin your day or your night.

Hold on to Your Values

Self-knowledge requires honesty and patience with yourself as you grow and change and learn. Know who you are and what matters to you so that you can decide where you best fit and how you can impress your working life with your personal values. You will live a stable and confident life if you are most true to yourself. If you are able to be consistent with your values, through the good times and even more in times of turmoil, your value to a company will grow, your sense of purpose and fulfillment will grow, and you will sleep better at night. A value match between you and the company you work for will make a huge, positive difference in your enjoyment quotient. We will discuss ways to investigate company and leadership values in Part II.

A value match between you and the company you work for will make a huge, positive difference in your enjoyment quotient.

Plan for the Rest of Your Life

Part of knowing yourself means knowing where your passions lie. It means knowing when you are the best you and making the needed provisions to reach that nirvana for yourself. Planning means keeping an eye on long-term, whole-life goals and keeping in tune with priority changes that will occur as you evolve through experiences in life and work. Keeping a wide view on opportunities will keep your ideas fresh and exciting and you might find ways to reach your working bliss that you hadn't thought of before. Money matters, and you need to start planning as soon as possible. Money is a big part of the freedom plan because it simply gives you the liberty from worry and bondage to a bad place. Having money will buy you time if you need it, or afford a life change if you want it. If you find that you are in a place that is not in concert with your values you will know it, and if you are prepared, you can make a positive change. This will be true in even the toughest times if you are excellent in your work, if you have the conviction to speak for your values, and if you are prepared financially to carry you over if you need it.

You can have it all even though there will be times when you can't have all of it at the same time. As circumstances and issues ebb and flow and you come to know yourself and believe in your convictions, you will weave your own rules. This might seem a tall order for some of you, but it is a reachable objective. You have the power. Take care of your reputation, ongoing education, integrity, and money. Own your career and stay true to yourself; don't let a career or company or someone's opinion of you own you. It is essential to understand the corporate objectives and it is your responsibility to gain that knowledge so that you can conquer difficulties in a way that is true to your values and sensibilities. It is your responsibility to let people know you and to understand the different styles and comfort zones of the hiring decision makers. The real work is about to begin.

> *Take care of your reputation, ongoing education, integrity, and money. Own your career and stay true to yourself; don't let a career or company or someone's opinion of you own you.*

QUESTIONS

The following questions might help you design and understand your own personal value kingdom. The answers are meant as a beginning for your own brainstorming session.

- **What is the real driver behind my desire to excel in my career?**
  Fulfillment, intellectual challenge, prestige, creative freedom, personal responsibilities, financial freedom, other?

■ **What makes me feel good in the workplace?**
Growth, feeling appreciated, making a difference, meeting objectives, creating new products, developing people, negotiation, believing I'm part of what makes the place tick, having information to move forward, winning, learning, impacting society, other?

■ **What sort of environment do I thrive in?**
Creative, open, smart colleagues, fast-paced, tough yet reachable challenges, great leadership, team spirit, opportunities for growth, belief in the product, other?

■ **What sort of environments upset me?**
Oppressive, closed, cliquey, noncreative, too pressurized, unrealistic goals, rude conduct, incompetent people, lack of integrity, weak leadership, hoarded information, few real opportunities for growth, not feeling like I'm a part in policy decisions, other?

■ **What makes me happy outside of my work life?**
Family, friends, love, art, music, working out, sports, travel, language, ocean and mountains, church, quiet, flowers, reading, inventing, yoga, other?

■ **What sort of person am I and do I want to be?**
High integrity, compassionate, creative, contributor, leader, respected, respectful, trusting, trustworthy, smart, stretched, successful, happy, fulfilled, generous, kind, always learning, curious, other?

■ **What personal goals do I have that I have yet to achieve?**
Financial freedom; being a great friend, son or daughter, sibling; a long-term relationship; marriage; parenting; running a marathon; learning Spanish; seeing Paris; owning my own business; other?

- How do I keep an eye on my personal value kingdom while I make kings for the corporation?

- How do I keep stress at bay so that I can accomplish my out-of-work-life needs and desires?

- How do I learn to understand business, navigate the road, and hold on to my core values?

3 A WORD ABOUT PROFIT

Businesses are for profit. If this notion is in any way new to you, or if you haven't realized the full weight of it, say it over and over again. The need to produce products that consumers will buy and to build environments that attract and retain great employees ultimately serves the profit motive. There is no judgment about this truth. Businesses don't stay in business if they don't pay full attention to growth, expenses, and the bottom line: profit.

Profit can be viewed as fuel for prosperity. Business is a main engine of our economy by keeping and creating jobs, and, through research and development, new products that enhance our quality of life and count toward our gross domestic product (GDP). Profit might be the company driver, but it also accounts for consumer confidence and major improvements in housing, incredible advances in medical care, organic or engineered foods on our tables, the contoured shoes on our feet, and so on.

Wall Street measures the value of a stock price, in part, by earnings projections met. The projections can be low, better if high, but the guidance from the company is paramount. The *guidance,* or forecast, reflects on the leadership of the company. It tells the world that the management at this company has its finger on the pulse of that industry and understands well how this company fits in its sector. An example of forecast guidance is "We project a 4 percent growth rate and earnings plus .50 in the second quarter." If the earnings projection is missed, by even a penny, the stock price is likely to go down. If it is missed, but management knows exactly why, and presents what it can do to fortify the future with fact-based authority, it will go down less, or not at all. If forecasts are missed on a regular basis, the CEO and CFO probably won't last.

Some experts view the unrelenting and unrealistic pressure for growth, as a basis for the price of a stock, to be a prominent reason for the recent spell of false reporting. Some companies are reconsidering the projection and reporting of earnings as a means to strengthen a stock price.

Coca-Cola surprised Wall Street with a change in forecasting policy in December 2002. As stated in the company press release, "The Company will no longer provide any quarterly or annual earnings per share guidance. . . . In the future, the Company will continue to provide investors with perspective on its value drivers, its strategic initiatives and those factors critical to understanding its business and operating environment. . . ."

Coca-Cola decided to take the pressure off earnings-per-share (EPS) projections to better concentrate on other "values, strategic initiatives, and operations" of the company. It will be interesting to watch if other companies follow them, or if this has any impact on the share price or even the profitability of Coca-Cola.

Does working for profit make the work seem less inviting? Some people have a difficult time with the idea of profit, believing it lessens the spirit or dignity of the work and the people who do it. Some people believe profit is the pure definition of greed, and negative headlines have only helped to feed that perception. Every company is not an Enron or WorldCom in the abusive sense, but every company is under pressure to produce profit.

New legislation and prosecution should guide the correction of problematic ethics in corporate America. The Sarbanes-Oxley Act of 2002, for instance, requires that CEOs and CFOs certify financial statements. Class action lawsuits such as Investors vs. Enron, criminal conviction of Arthur Andersen LLP, and the prosecution against leaders such as Jeffrey Skilling, and Andrew Fastow from Enron and others will serve as a warning to all corporations. It is hoped that ethics and leadership issues will straighten out, but the pursuit of profit will not cease.

Understanding finance is an imperative if you want to grow into a position of real importance to the company. It would be a good idea to check your human resources department to see if any classes such as "Finance for Non-Financials" are available, through the company, to enhance your knowledge. You might also check your local colleges and other adult education resources. Gaining analytical skills and building familiarity with finance and accounting rules and terminology will increase your value, and it will also widen your comfort zone in this critical area of business. This knowledge will help you to understand the underlying considerations that go into the decisions made about everything from capacity to new product rollouts to headcount. Pressure to make sales budgets or to contain costs is forced by projected expenses and how they fit with the profit goals of the company. You need fluency in the language of finance if you are ever going to run a company.

> *Gaining analytical skills and building familiarity with finance and accounting rules and terminology will increase your value, and it will also widen your comfort zone in this critical area of business.*

The way leaders lead makes a difference in the company culture and its relative perspective on profit. Your interest in the stock price might be based on long-term personal security issues such as your 401(k) or pension plan. Because you can choose to direct your investments into company stock, you might be more interested in where the price sits, but do you also think about your impact on the stock? There are many ways that you can affect the company margin from any position; examples will be found in Part II and throughout the book.

Consciousness of the profit goal is advised as a way for each person in the workforce to see his or her part as a contributor to the company's overriding objective. By understanding this largest goal—profit—and working in a way that plugs into it, you become more and more valuable to the place. Your insight is deeper and your work takes on an added dimension. At the very least, understanding why you have a budget to make or stay within will make more sense to you.

FIND THE GOOD

There is absolute meaning and purpose to go along with the profit goal. Find the meaning in your job so that you can wrap yourself in it and feel fine about the larger prospect. I used to contemplate how my job in television stacked up in terms of contributions to humanity. I sometimes felt that we sold products, through advertising, that people didn't really need or couldn't really afford. I came to realize that our industry contributed to the country's GDP and by helping to create competition in the marketplace, we helped to build consumer confidence and competition that could lead to lower prices. I respected television for its community outreach and dedication to information and education. I liked program offerings that simply made people think, laugh, cry, relax, and gather together. I was able to find and advocate for good in the product of television. What is the good in your product or service? ∎

Meaning can come from the way your company aids or improves society or in the form of the product you help to produce and position in the marketplace. Meaning can come in the jobs that impact production and in the security for the people who fill them. Mentoring and developing talent to grow people into better and more gratified employees can help you to derive purpose. Meaning and purpose can be found when you expend your own creative energies to make a boring job more exciting or to develop ideas that become new strategies or products. Creating efficiencies that improve the workplace will serve to simplify your life. There are many ways to find meaning and fulfillment from your corner of the world, and they are all wrapped inside the profit envelope.

The profit picture does not have to take away from your enjoyment or sense of fulfillment. A movie director wants to make a great film, but he understands it has to make money for the studio or he might not get work again so easily. An actor wants to perform in a great role, but she understands that audiences must want to see her on the screen or she might not get the next role. Money drives business and at one place or another, it affects every one of us. Make friends with the notion, understand it, and do your part, cocooned within your own mission.

QUESTIONS

- How do you feel about profit as a main company driver?

- How can contributing to profit enhance your sense of purpose and/or fulfillment?

- What is the greater good in your product or service?

- What personal profit, besides money, can you derive from your invested efforts? What components of your job drive and feed your passions?

- Do you find you are more likely to invest time and care when you are most passionate about something?

- Do you believe that being passionate about your work makes profit more palatable and easier to achieve?

4 POLITICS AT LARGE

Politics at the workplace are real, insidious and mostly unsettling. Politics are easily half of your job even if you think you're not political. You can opt out, be an astute moderate, or be a political animal. Politics is the art and science of gaining "inside" access to the top people and positions in the organization. Even if you opt out of the maneu-

Politics are easily half of your job even if you think you're not political.

vers, you are affected by politics because it impacts your peer group, your leadership and the whole flavor of the place. If you are a moderate, you are astute enough to understand the game and gain some level of appeal and respect, but probably not driven enough to attain total membership in the "club" and a seat at the big table. If you are a political animal, your rise might seem easier because you have aligned yourself with the legitimate powers that be, perhaps comfortably and possibly at some cost to your integrity.

Politics is difficult to think about, let alone live and deal with. All you have to do is read the political news and business papers or watch CNBC and you can see the drama for yourself. The jockeying for positions is blatant, as is the cronyism involved in placing people in high-level posts. You watch and listen as politicians and business leaders spin ambivalent facts into positive, authoritative sound bites that they hope you will believe completely and not investigate further. An example of spin is one that you might see often on television. The claim is "Channel XXX . . . Your News Leader." The fact is that the station won a ratings contest in the marketplace. The spin is that the lead might be in only one or two demographics, although the claim would have you believe the station is the market leader across the board.

People like to hire people they know. Know what? Know that directives will be followed. Know that you think as they think and behave as they behave. Know that you all understand who "gets in" and who doesn't. Know that everyone wants to be in your club and that makes you special. Know what? It's real, it's powerful, it's exclusive, and it can be very disheartening to some.

Politics took a lot of the joy out of my work. Politics and the acceptance of behavior and attitudes that were repugnant to my personal value system helped me decide to leave my career. Let me explain. The higher you go the tougher it gets. People are jockeying for fewer positions and ruthless behavior can rule the day. Overt war takes shape and it is placed on your desk and in your throat via memo or a confrontation with an angst-driven colleague. The club rules become more hard-line, and the necessary sponsorship more elusive. There is a silent knowledge of the rules of the club, and unless you know the rules and decide to play by them, you can't get in. You can't know the rules to abide by unless someone brings you inside or you are a very good listener and observer. It seems the choice is between spending your energies gaining inclusion or continuing to take pleasure in the creation and delivery of great work and ride through it, or somewhere in between. Sometimes the middle ground is the best place because you can be yourself and achieve great results and gratification while you grow your own agency and security.

> *You can't know the rules to abide by unless someone brings you inside or you are a very good listener and observer.*

I entered the phrase "corporate politics" into an online bookseller's search engine and a myriad of titles came shooting at me: *Eat or Be Eaten, Swim with the Sharks, The Secret Handshake, Winning Office Politics, Games Bosses Play, Dealing With People You Can't Stand*, and on and on. All of these books, and many more, tell us of the unavoidable political treachery that is attached to our jobs. Clearly, a challenge to conquer. I want to try to clarify a course where you can keep yourself intact and be wildly successful in spite of, or in tandem with, politics. There are no one-size-fits-all generic answers. The answer is to understand the game and make your own choices about how deeply you are able or willing to entrench yourself before it costs you your values or your sense of self.

Here's what happens. Powerful people get to be powerful because they are bright, visionary, charismatic, disciplined and well connected. People want to be near them, work for them, and learn from them. This awareness is aphrodisiacal and makes the powerful ones want more. They surround themselves with people who keep their personal power systems stoked and they include this group in their politics and strategic planning. They share in the execution of work that services the company and their careers. The danger is that this creates an ivory tower where the king is no longer in touch with the court because the people with the king aren't paying attention to those below.

> Powerful people get to be powerful because they are bright, visionary, charismatic, disciplined and well connected. People want to be near them, work for them, and learn from them.

The power group is notorious; everyone knows who they are. They eat together and stand together at cocktail parties. They form a wall around themselves and open the door in kindly gestures at group gatherings. They know everybody's name and walk around with heads up and smiles bright. They're generally nice and polite as they walk through the hallways; they can afford to be courteous because they are the elite and the envied and maybe even the hated and they don't care because they're in and you wannabe.

Do you want to be? Do you want to be included in the group that makes things happen? You want to be a major contributor and these are the people who get it done. You don't want your work to be hidden or claimed by another because you want your voice heard and your work, which represents you, to matter. On the other hand, you don't necessarily want to be like them because you might not like or trust them. So, the challenge is to be accepted on the merits of your work and the style that is your own, without taking on the negative aspects of the pack. It can be done.

Most likely, these achievers are smart, good, likeable people in and of themselves, but the pack mentality and activity makes them seem ugly at times. It is wise not to give the pack the power over your own self-assessment and it might be helpful to appeal to one person at a time rather than the whole group. This is a personal game as much as it is a business one. It is not only about the work; in some cases your style might not be to their liking.

This is a personal game as much as it is a business one. It is not only about the work; in some cases your style might not be to their liking.

Perhaps you are a questioner or unwilling to be complacent even in good times. Perhaps you are uncomfortable to be around because you are different from the power group in some tangible way.

The decision to adapt to become part of an exclusive group might have its genesis in feelings from a much earlier part of your life. Maybe you craved popularity, or wanted to be the president of the class or valedictorian. Maybe you strived to be the star athlete or the student council president that everyone wanted to be around. Maybe you wanted to be approved of and included, or you just wanted to be part of the action. Maybe you shunned it all and got attention for being different and this isn't happening now. As an adult in the work world you might think you *need* to matter more than you really even *want* to matter to these folks.

NOBODY'S BETTER THAN YOU

Depending on who you are and your personal experience, this approval need will vary. I was lucky to have parents who instilled a sense of self-worth in my siblings and me. My dad looked me in the eye one day when I was fairly young and said, "Joanne, you're going to go out into the world and meet many different types of people. Some will have more money than you'll ever dream of. Some will have degrees or titles that you won't even understand. Some will have fancy clothes and fancy cars. Joanne, stand tall and look anyone in the eye because you are as rich as any of them because you are loved."

Some of you might think this is simplistic, but I promise you that these words saved me in many, many intimidating situations. What can you take from your own life that can give you confidence? Perhaps it is in your own family life, or track record in business or volunteerism, or perhaps it is in the honor of your good work and integrity. This conviction can free you from needing the approval of just *anyone* in power in order to feel good about your work or yourself. Use your own informed judgment to decide who you respect most and let those people's opinions matter to you.

I did not want to be part of a club that included people who were mean-spirited or excluded people who could offer great competencies but weren't cool enough by some subjective criteria. I heard the "clubbers" talk about people behind their backs because these folks were comfortable speaking freely in front of me. They hadn't counted on the fact that I would stand up for many of the people they shot down, and I didn't count on being labeled as "about the people," as if that were a bad thing. ■

If you are working alone and someone enters the room, the dynamic changes. Add a third and a fourth person and it changes that many more times. Add a senior executive and it changes exponentially. This way of life is magnified in the office. Many people worry about the manager's perceptions of them, so they are not at ease giving their opinions candidly. Your colleague might confide that he or she doesn't agree with a certain protocol and then act in a completely opposite manner, in line with the boss's thinking. I likened this to a breach of truth and found my choices were to make my thoughts known or to avoid the conversation completely. Most often I would speak my truth to my manager and offer suggestions, but I would ultimately comply with his or her direction. I had the personal comfort of knowing that I tried to give a different view on the subject and that I was true to myself as well as my work obligations.

Politics were tough for me, probably because of my own attitude toward them and because I didn't have a mentor to show me the way. I thought it meant changing me or sublimating my belief system, and I thought it meant I had to insincerely "kiss up." I thought it meant lying about who I was and what I thought. I knew it was smart to be aware of the expected answer, but I wanted the freedom and the open environment to disagree if necessary. I

> *I knew it was smart to be aware of the expected answer, but I wanted the freedom and the open environment to disagree if necessary.*

thought kissing up demeaned me and actually was a sign of disrespect to my manager and the company. I believed a dignified way to work was to be a knowledgeable worker and thinker with a positive mental attitude and a will to win. I most respected people who were thinkers rather than reactors. I wanted managers and leaders who enjoyed hearing different angles and innovative thought. I often asked questions about communication style and innovation in the interviewing process because I wanted to know if I was going to report to someone who wanted new and different or who was interested in protecting the status quo. I was lucky to have some managers who enjoyed contribution and I felt stifled by others who didn't.

As an astute moderate, I came to realize that it is imperative to success, and perhaps to a sense of fulfillment and gratification, to have the people who matter know you and your contributions. This is Mission Impossible unless you are open to interacting comfortably with them. It is essential that you figure out why you are uneasy about politics if you are. Do you feel intimidated by the people you'd have to get to know? Do you feel strong and secure about your contributions? Do you believe you have something to offer? Do you have anything in common with these people beyond your workplace? Do you dislike them or distrust them for any rational reason?

I think I felt a bit intimidated and I also think that I found them slightly boorish and boring and so pumped up on their own self-love that I didn't want to contribute further; maybe this was a defensive reverse-club action on my part. In any case, it might help you to always remember that you are in the organization because of your competencies and promise in the first place. These powers saw something in you that they could grow to mutual benefit and satisfaction.

> *It might help you to always remember that you are in the organization because of your competencies and promise in the first place.*

A good friend in a very high place told me her views on intimidation: "One of the reasons that managing up is so difficult for me is that I tend to think that the manager must be "better" than I am—more knowledgeable, competent, grounded, balanced. In fact, I hope they are, since that would satisfy the basic craving that there is somebody to lean on . . . it is why you want a strong president—there is a sense of safety if the person in charge is charismatic and competent. So, without careful consideration, I attribute these characteristics and create my own intimidating boss."

Creating our own intimidating boss is something that we all probably do at one time or another. We believe our leaders are omnipotent, and how can that be comfortable?

I strongly advise that you get to know what makes you uncomfortable about politics and work to break this down enough so that it is not an obstacle for you. I believed my purpose was above the politics and I drove through walls on merit, daring and humor.

At varying times in my career I felt the friction of the club wall and perhaps it wasn't so unique; maybe the tension was an intentional "separation vibration" that the intrepid leaders sent my way, or maybe it was my own insecure invention. You would think that the higher the rank the lesser the apprehension, but this was not the case for me, and it is still not always the case for many of my still-engaged former colleagues. The trick is to go on with your work and feign that you are in that group; you will learn soon enough if you've crossed a boundary or need to improve on any important competencies. Keep moving on, believe in your work and your worth, and let the results speak with a higher volume than your actual voice. I relied heavily on the results and dignity of my work, my direct manager and my peer group for support and motivation, and most of the time I was okay. It took me too long to realize that even though I believed I had something important to offer, some managers wouldn't always be happy to hear from me.

Believe in your work and your worth, and let the results speak with a higher volume than your actual voice.

The big picture answers are within you and you will discover what sits right for you. Let your own inner voice be your guide. Listen to yourself while you listen to those around you. Listen and observe, be aware, and be prepared.

QUESTIONS

- How do you feel about politics in general?

- Do you identify yourself as an opt out, astute moderate, or political animal?

- Are you comfortable with your political identity or would you like to make a shift? Which way?

- Are you able to see the political reality and work through it in peace with your core values?

- What can you do to make yourself more comfortable in the company of leaders and vice versa?

5 POLITICS IN THE DAY TO DAY

BE YOURSELF AND STILL GIVE THEM WHAT THEY WANT

You can remain yourself and give your boss what he or she needs while you are building relationships with these important players in the organization. Think about what they want, why they want it, how they want it and when. Ask questions if you don't have the information to deliver stellar work that begs no question. Most leaders love to teach and enjoy speaking from their experiences and points of view. If you don't agree with them, at least you will understand. You can deliver the work as requested while including your own ideas in a style that might find easier acceptance.

Think about what they want, why they want it, how they want it and when.

Your work will speak for itself, but your champions will speak, too. You have to let the important people know who you are, what makes you tick, where you want to go, and why you can do it. Your manager and champion must believe in you so that you will be top of mind and they will advocate for you without thinking twice. Understanding the company goals, your king's goals, and your own goals will go a long way to expedite your career growth.

This is a two-pronged proposition. The first and possibly easiest approach is to deliver notable work in the manner requested. Think of your manager and those above him or her as your greatest customers. By understanding their stress and style you will be informed about the best way to approach the person with your ideas and goals. Is your manager social or analytical? Intense or laid back? Is he or she a big-picture thinker or glued to the smaller view of the specific goal? Deliver your intentions in the manager's style and you will be closer to a win–win result.

Be consistently well prepared in meetings. Know your material and the attending ancillary data that supports your viewpoints. Think beyond the normal zone; anticipate all angles of the problem so that you can offer unique solutions to the obstacles.

Think big . . . Put your head in your manager's head and understand the greater goal that your task is a part of. Perhaps you will come up with an innovative suggestion that will hit the objective and the larger view right on target. Understanding why someone needs something helps you to perceive the company better and the way the leaders think, impress, win, and matter in the organization. Grasp what is important to the company and become involved in those projects if you can.

The second level, the personal and social, is equally important. If a manager has a choice between two people with equal competencies, the person he or she is most comfortable with will win. Comfort zone has to do with trust and compatibility in values, passions, vision and style, decision-making processes, and communications. The hiring manager needs to know that he or she can make a mistake or say something off the cuff that will not come back to haunt him or her. The leader needs to believe in the ultimate trustworthiness of the candidate. Trust of this sort comes with time, and that is one more reason to let yourself and your work be known earlier rather than later. The social aspect might even include something as basic as being able to enjoy your company over a meal or other off-hours activities.

If a manager has a choice between two people with equal competencies, the person he or she is most comfortable with will win.

If the friendlier, better personally known and more trusted of the candidates has fewer competencies but is a quick study, the hiring manager might choose to suffer the immediate ramp-up time for the long-term comfort zone. Some leaders want to move on their agendas with the least possible resistance. Ramp-up time on a process is easier than building a new relationship because process is not personal: You can get from A to B more quickly with someone who already knows the way you want to attack a project, and it's even faster when philosophies are in sync.

Success is in what you know and do, but it is greatly influenced by who knows you. Take opportunities at social functions to speak to these key stakeholders on a quasi-personal level. Seek them out at internal company functions and introduce them to your customers at external events. This was not the easiest thing for me, but I pushed myself to be open and as seemingly comfortable as possible in this arena. My wariness is still an interesting proposition, considering I could work a room of customers, peers, and the people who reported to me with the best of them. I chalk it up to being astute enough to understand that one wrong word or action could harm me more than one great joke or insight could help me. I also believe I was circumstantially shy; I encourage you to take steps to overcome this if you are, too.

Push yourself to let people know you as a person as well as a worker. I learned a great lesson in an acting class that worked very well in many situations. Prepare yourself mentally before an event by picturing yourself as the person you'd like to be seen as. Think about the competencies and personal qualities you'd like to portray and think of a person or object in the universe that has these qualities. Become that character for the length of the meeting, presentation, or gathering. The visualization will help you to be more comfortable bearing these characteristics, which you own anyway. You are not being phony, because this is really an exercise in exposing a true part of you that is normally saved for people you feel more at ease with. It would mean assuming a comfort zone, convincing yourself to be confident and relaxed, so that you can show your truest self to the world at large while still respecting the boundaries and styles of each targeted person. It's not so far removed from the way you'd like to be on any first meeting with someone: comfortable, humorous, informed, provocative, and a good listener. Leave the people, with whom you interact on this level, wanting more.

Be smart and act with common sense. Although you might be free to brainstorm and disagree in your workplace, disagree with respect. Don't get overly excited and fight with others, especially a manager, in front of others, and don't make your arguments personal. If you see that your manager, or a colleague has made an error, bring it to him or her personally rather than possibly embarrassing that person in front of a group. If this happens while you're in a large meeting, slip a note, or notify by computer messaging if that is more appropriate. Be smart in your delivery as you aid your manager, all the while understanding the goal, the players and the surroundings. Remember to save your manager from embarrassment whenever possible.

> *Although you might be free to brainstorm and disagree in your workplace, disagree with respect.*

THE ALLIANCE DANCE

For many years I naively thought meetings were about the agenda on the paper. I also believed that decisions were made in meetings, rather than in get-togethers before or after the meeting. The topics might seem obvious, but sometimes the real reasons for a meeting are hidden, so prepare with care.

Once, when I was working for a network-owned television station, the company was taken over by another and such a meeting occurred. I had been with this station for two years and had been promoted to a new position only months before the takeover. It was the case of a smaller company taking over a classic network and the smaller company was insinuating its culture quickly, overtly and in a conquering (not assimilating) manner.

The top three sales executives came over to our station to meet with the general manager and our top two sales executives (including me). I came to the meeting with suggestions for the national sales firm. We were severely understaffed, large advertising budgets were up and our market revenue shares were miserable. I had several examples of work I considered below standard and offered solutions in the form of staffing, training and customer relations. My general manager called me defensive as he interrupted me in the middle of my presentation. I was caught off guard because my intention was to be proactive and *offensive;* to my mind I was not playing defense. I was aghast, deflated and perplexed. In hindsight, I realize that I simply didn't get it. I did not understand the real agenda at the time, which was to rub elbows, become friendly and agree to work together in the new company way with no waves of change in the offing. The meeting was political, but I thought it was about creating a better workplace. If I had it to do over again, I would have asked my direct manager what the real agenda was. I probably would still have come prepared with suggested improvements, but the timing and tone might have been very different on my part. That meeting marked me as a problem to the new management and I felt it. I decided to leave the company within that year.

The topics might seem obvious, but sometimes the real reasons for a meeting are hidden, so prepare with care.

These sorts of meetings always unsettled my stomach because I thought they were gratuitous and phony and not about the work. This type of meeting is the ultimate alliance dance, where words belie the actions and the real drama. I can only wonder now if I had been more astute going in, would I have even offered my suggestions and solutions? Would it have bothered me less if my expectations had been in line? Could I have been more okay with the fact that business takes a back seat to politics some of the time, or that politics does move business along? The only way for me to get around this would have been to understand the real agenda and approach it as theater: Get on the stage, perform, and get off, waiting for the correct opportunity to make the case you want heard. If you

can manage to integrate your business goals into the understood forums, you will have an easier time of it. This sort of situation begs this question: How can you affect positive change
when no one wants to hear your ideas? You wait for the right
time while using the proper channels. If you're not sure of time
or place, ask your manager for advice. If your deeply held
beliefs are ignored after you finally have the opportunity to
present and discuss them, you'll have to decide if you can
work for the long term with people whose stance is to protect
the status quo, or not to look for better processes.

MANAGING CHANGE AND TIMING

Some people think about their next job as soon as they're
in a new one. They begin immediately to align new "sponsors"
and expend energy on their own career rather then the work,
something like a politician who lives by the polls and begins a
reelection campaign nearly as soon as the election is over. I
always thought these people cheated themselves and the people they worked for a bit. I didn't see that they could very well
enjoy the place they were in, improve it, and learn from the
position if their heads were always in the future.

You need to excel in each step of your career to be ready
and able to handle the next one. If you are in a constant hurry,
there will be a day when you reach your own level of incompetence. Moving too fast could deny you
the skill sets and perspective you need

> *You need to excel in each step of your career to be ready and able to handle the next one.*

to lead. Take your time and enjoy yourself while keeping an eye (rather than
your whole mind) on your next or long-
term goal.

Remember that companies are for profit and although you
might be treasured, respected and even well liked, you are, in
the end, a tool to make profit. You are a chess piece maneuvered
by the master for the good of the company's growth and often
his or her own growth as well. Do your part and enjoy yourself,
but try not to have the illusion that this is some substitute or

second family. You are an employee because you are useful and probably pleasant enough to be around. No one is indispensable and "soft skills" such as leadership and motivational skills can't be measured easily.

Changes in ownership and leadership can also create a change in focus and energy. My best advice here is to keep your head down and continue to deliver substantive work. Be an aid to the incoming leadership and try to avoid the angst of others. Do not join in the gossip if you can help it, and do your best to keep a positive mental attitude through the change. Let the people who manage speak for you until such time that you can ask for your own meeting, if that is appropriate. Be a professional and let your work and reputation precede you in a positive way. It usually will.

The rumor mill will be working quadruple overtime in times of change. Rumors will only help to create and increase angst, as security is replaced by fear, which puts people into a *survive*, rather than *thrive* mode. It can be very harmful to a person's credibility and to your organization's reputation when the rumors include specific names of people who are being conjectured to lose their job or be promoted at someone else's expense. If you are inundated with this environment, it might be a very good idea to take the rumors to your manager. If you are the manager, you should address the group and quash the rumors. It is even acceptable to say you don't know what the outcome of the changes will be, or that you cannot say more than you can. The message and leadership will be clear: All hands need to stay on deck and forward movement cannot cease. The people who work for you will appreciate your effort and if you are able to clear the air, all will benefit. People need leadership in times of change, not rumors and innuendo.

People need leadership in times of change, not rumors and innuendo.

If you are in a company where you do not admire upper management and their philosophical and managerial tenets, you are in a tough spot. If the politics of the place reward action you do not agree with and consistently promote people whose values are not the same, or even close to your own, you could be headed for some unhappy times. I had to feel good about the purpose of the place and the action of its leaders or I experienced an actual internal dissonance. I was not happy in a place where the sociology was inconsistent, mean-spirited, or closed. I loved the work but always hated the negative, territorial, exclusive political environments that seemed to thrive at times, even in companies that espoused a greater vision.

All too often, a company can have a well-intentioned charter or mission statement that is not brought to life by the leaders who manage people and environments. This is simply regrettable because the greatest of intentions can become the "Big Lie" and might leave the employee feeling cheated, fooled, orphaned and ready to leave. Retention of the A player might depend on being an included stakeholder of a mission or charter statement. Living a lie won't sit well with people of high integrity. The company leaders must find ways to ensure that the company charter is lived and led by the people in positions to do so. You can do your part in keeping a value statement alive by standing up for the espoused beliefs whenever you see a breach.

THE TRICKSTER

Tricksters believe they have the game down. These are the people who come to work 15 minutes before the boss each day so that they appear to have been there much longer. These are the people who write e-mails from home to show the date and time stamp because that matters more to them than any message they send in the text. Tricksters are the people who do not prepare for a meeting and have the nerve to hook on to your hard work with a pithy line and a grin.

People who smile to everyone's face and have a sarcastic, sexist, or racist remark behind their backs are tricksters. These are the yes-people who do what they want anyway, or never stand up for their beliefs if they differ from that of their boss. Maybe they don't have any beliefs besides working for their own promotion, or a desire to keep their high-paying, safe-haven job. These are the people who disagree with everything just to be heard, or call you on mistakes in front of others to look smarter. The tricksters are more likely to gossip than others are, and often start rumors in which they star. Their actions are insidious and they believe they have it all figured out because for some, it works. It works because the hiring and promoting manager likes this person enough and the work is "good enough." The trickster might get by because the manager does not see the duplicitous side of his or her personality and believes the trickster to be in sync with the value criteria of the specific job and the place as a whole.

What to do? First, believe and hope that if you see it others do, too. Slacking and cheating on the job are transparent and even the most charming individual can get away with it for only so long. If you are in a situation where someone steals your work in a meeting, ask your manager if he or she saw what the person did, or go to the culprit directly and ask that this not be repeated. It might not happen to you again. In the long run, the trickster might not be fired, but he or she might not get promoted or given additional growth challenges either.

> *Slacking and cheating on the job are transparent and even the most charming individual can get away with it for only so long.*

What if the trickster is your boss? A person I know had an experience in publishing, in which his immediate superior took informative memos he wrote to her, deleted his name and passed the memo on to her boss. Her boss thought the ideas were so good that he copied and circulated the memo to all with a handwritten note complimenting her for being so up to date. What could my friend do in this situation, beyond having the delicious knowledge that his boss knew that he knew what she was made of? Choices include the following:

- Accept this reality and realize that you get paid to do a great job and the manager takes credit and is assigned blame.
- Discuss your displeasure with your manager, explaining that, for you, attribution motivates innovation and contribution.

- Let it slip somehow to the higher-up that you were happy the action was appreciated.
- Try to eventually work in an area that this person does not control.

This is a crushing reality and it happens all the time. It could break trust and propel you to leave an otherwise good company. I've had repeated situations in my career when a superior took an idea and made it his or her own, or took credit for sales objectives met that he or she had absolutely nothing to do with. Bad bosses abound, and many leaders believe that anything that comes from the group that reports to him or her can be put to work to enrich their own careers. Attribution scares the trickster because he or she is insecure or guilty enough about his or her own contribution (or lack thereof) and does not want to highlight people who could be deemed the better innovator.

What if the trickster is your boss?

I was actually laughed at once, in a meeting with a divisional president, for giving attribution for some great ideas. I suppose it happened enough that at one meeting he rolled his eyes at the others in the group and then looked at me and said, "You don't have to do that you know, this isn't high school." I was astonished and dumbfounded, and noted that some of the people in the room chuckled along, sycophantically. I answered that I thought he might want to know who the bright lights on the floor were. To me, this attitude encouraged credit taking as the standard and I thought that was unfortunate for our culture. I didn't admire this leadership but I didn't want to make this difference a pivotal issue between us. I kept giving credit where it was due, and he finally stopped rolling his eyes.

There will always be tricky bosses . . . more on this in Part II.

QUESTIONS

- Do you try to overcome shyness or intimidation so that the people who matter know you?

- Do you have people that you can trust to ask about real agendas?

- Can you lead in a way that is open and honest regardless of the politics?

- Can you lead in a way that brings a company charter to life even if your immediate boss does not?

- Are you fearless and relentless in asking questions or making positive suggestions?

- Can you discuss or even argue without getting personal?

- Are you comfortable with good enough or do you strive for the best possible scenario?

- Are you able to promote yourself and your work in a way that you find acceptable?

- Are you a trickster?

- How do you relate to tricksters, especially if one is your direct boss?

6 LOSING LIKE A WINNER

Noticing political behavior in others that win promotions can be disheartening as you realize that charades are often accepted as reality. Sometimes people who don't seem to deserve a promotion get one for reasons you might not see, such as going to a competitor, which could embarrass or hurt your company. Remember to always think beyond the obvious. Also realize that high-level management probably does not see some of the conduct you question in your assessment of the individual. Many times kings will take their makers along to continue the service of their own objectives, and this is a formidable problem if you are not one of them.

> *Sometimes people who don't seem to deserve a promotion get one for reasons you might not see, such as going to a competitor, which could embarrass or hurt your company.*

Many times you will witness the Peter Principle in action. A person who has been a yes-man for his or her entire career suddenly becomes the leader. This person, who has hardly ever had an original thought, is the leader of a division that impacts you specifically. When people of this type are elevated they will either be smart and courageous enough to hire their own kingmakers, even if they are smarter and more hardworking than themselves, or they will hire a similar suit to control and appear to be smarter than. In any case, time will prove what this new leader is made of; if it is the worst-case scenario, you have a shot at outliving their reign.

If you don't get a promotion you believe you deserve, handle yourself with dignity. The way you lose often counts for more than the way you win. Ask for clarity and search for lessons you can learn so that you aren't disappointed the next time. Take a deep breath and recount the interviews you had in your job pursuit and see where you could have improved the case for your efficacy. Take a second deep breath and see if you can understand that not getting the job might be in your best long-term interest. If getting a job you want, and believe you deserve, means having to work for someone you don't believe in, what is the ultimate cost to you? You are better off working in a situation where you are compatible and comfortable with the person to whom you report. Believe this and feel good about who you are and where you are, doing your part to make your current position a place of high contribution and profile. You can't win them all, and hopefully you work beside intelligent, hardworking, deserving people. "Losing" to a qualified rival will help to make you feel better about a situation and yourself if you can be objective. Learn from it, accept it, and move on.

> If getting a job you want, and believe you deserve, means having to work for someone you don't believe in, what is the ultimate cost to you?

Sometimes, moving on means leaving the company, and this is a very serious issue. There is much to consider: Will it be different anywhere else? Will the time it takes to develop a reputation inside the new company be longer than another opportunity in your current company? Do you respect and trust your company and its leadership? Do you enjoy your work overall? Can you see why you didn't get the job and believe those answers to be honorable (although difficult)? Are there important style differences or competencies that you still need to work on? Do you respect the person who won over you? Can you stay in your workplace, continue to contribute, and have another opportunity in your company? Will changing companies hurt your overall marketability and career goals? Are you going to something better and more compatible with your values or are you leaving because you are angry?

I had what I considered to be two serious promotion "losses" for jobs that I knew I could have handled and believed I had earned.

The first was a situation at a television station where I was second in line in the sales department, reporting to a manager I respected and cared for, but who, due to wild circumstances, ran the department rather dysfunctionally. There was serious infighting between him and his boss, our general manager. She came to us from another industry and her first day in TV was as our GM. She was open to, and full of, new ideas and wanted to bring new competencies and measurements to our company; she charged us to be innovative and to "not think like a television station." One of her greatest mandates was that we accept her as the conductor while we continually developed new "sheet music" in the form of new ideas that would bring our station to the number one position in the New York market. This general manager was innovative and daring and enjoyed working in chaos with several different high-priority tasks in the works at one time. It wasn't always easy, but it was exciting and new. My manager did not want to entertain changes that would affect the sales and marketing of the television station and as a result he was not overly interested in educating her about our business or our systems. He often avoided her by being out of the office when she needed him and I became his enabler, covering for him when he was "unavailable." I would attend meetings and dutifully report every word that he missed. He loved me for covering for him, but he hated me for covering for him. It was awful and hellish and the push–pull lasted for a few years.

> *Are you going to something better and more compatible with your values or are you leaving because you are angry?*

Although I was often in distress over the dysfunction, I learned a lot in the process. I was able to go beyond the role of my normal function and work with every other area of the television station. After a few years of learning and change amidst major chaos, my manager left and our general manager was moved to another area in the company. Our new general manager brought in a protégé from the outside to be the general sales manager and I was not promoted to the post that I had worked toward, and one I had helped to manage behind the scenes for six years. I was never given a real reason for this loss, but in many ways it was obvious. Our new GM wanted her own people in place. Sales and finance are two of the most important areas at a TV station and the jobs are generally filled with competent people that the GM can trust (or control). The GM didn't have, or take, the time to know me, or perhaps I was too entrenched as a leader of the old regime, enjoying strong relationships with the other departments, and specifically the crucial sales department.

I faced a serious dilemma when I was not promoted. I was bruised from the many years of dysfunction at the station and I was very upset that my new GM didn't take the time to know me. I was disturbed that the higher officers of the company did not advocate harder for me. I realized later that I might have been widely supported for the post, but as a general rule the leader of a place gets to choose his or her own team. I knew that if I wanted to grow in the company I'd have to leave New York for a different market because this post was now closed for a number of years. I decided to go to a career counselor for guidance before simply jumping ship. I was advised to pause and use the place as a healing and rest stop if I could live with the new management. They were hardworking people, and pleasant enough to be around, so I took that tack and stayed on for a year after the disappointment. I rested and healed and continued to contribute until a new realization developed that we did not have compatible business philosophies. I struggled and fought for my positions and ultimately decided that my attachment to the values I held high in business and my repu-tation in the market were more important to me than chang-ing valuable principles to stay on. I left that television station after nearly seven years of superb wins and learning and strug-gle and change. I went to Malta, where I have family and friends, for a month of clear respite. I challenged myself to "live in the now" and I worked hard on understanding my identity beyond businessperson . . . good lessons both. I went directly to the ocean on returning and after a few weeks more, landed a management job at a different television station in the New York market.

The second big loss hurt differently. I was part of a three-person team to open and operate, from scratch, an in-house national rep firm for an owned-station division of a major network. We built a nirvana and kept it for nearly three years. We created an environment that you mostly only dream about. We worked with the sales leaders from the television stations to create a team charter dedicated to excellence in work and communication. We believed in the charter and we lived it, protected it, and breathed life into it everyday. We hired A players with the simple, verbal contract that our group came to work each day with a dedication to very high standards and the clear objective to grow share and revenue for our television stations. What the workforce received in return was an environment where they didn't have to worry about pay structure, vacations, or what mood their boss was in. They were safe to disagree and make suggestions for a better process or place. The people who worked in our organization were treated with respect, as adults and managers of their business. We went from 0 to 60 in no time and the place hummed.

I had become my boss's go-to person and I was regularly rewarded with more work. I didn't mind because I loved the place, the company, and the learning. I received excellent training and had challenge and opportunity in an environment that was positive and thriving. My manager was promoted and I made a pitch for his job after much thought and soul searching. I was honestly not sure that I wanted the role because our business was changing, the job required ridiculously more hours than even I put in at the time, and the president who I'd report to was very analytical and hands on. We had very different personalities and styles. On the other hand, I was a key architect in the company. I was at senior vice president level, the number two in the rep organization, and I wouldn't have to leave New York for the promotion. I could handle the job and I believed I was the heir apparent. My key personal hurdles were the time and pressure commitment that

> *I had become my boss's go-to person and I was regularly rewarded with more work. I didn't mind because I loved the place, the company, and the learning. I received excellent training and had challenge and opportunity in an environment that was positive and thriving.*

would be necessary to do the job well and a style compatibility situation with the person I would report to. In the end I decided to go for it regardless of the demands and the risks.

After nearly four months of "dress rehearsal," meaning that I continued to do my work and integrate my promoted boss's role as well, I did not get the job. I went to many meetings with the president for regular business and had several off-site interviews for the post. My competition was a well-experienced, well-championed, politically savvy, smart, hard-working and likeable sales executive from one of our TV stations. I asked for feedback after hearing that I was not to be promoted and my request was denied. The president said he was not going to sit there and tell me the good and bad things about my competitor and me. My competitor was now my new boss, the newest king in waiting, and I received no input on why I didn't get the job.

I reported dutifully to my new manager and we generally got along. Here we went again: I had the institutional knowledge and he had the job. I honestly viewed him as an equal and wondered often why I wasn't promoted. We agreed on business in many ways and could even finish each other's sentences. The differences that emerged represented a cultural shift constituted by a grave difference in attitudes about environment, objectives, and people. He said that he was about results and I was about people. I argued that the results had been fantastic, and they started and ended with the people. I enjoyed and fostered environments built on open communication, respect and trust versus a more autocratic approach built on the intimidating and closed notion of "my way or the highway." I valued our employee base and believed in retaining and growing them versus the belief that people are easily replaceable. I'd heard often, behind closed doors and throughout my career, "If they don't like it here they can leave."

Although I was very disappointed and my head spun with unanswered questions, I didn't think about quitting then. I had a great deal of respect for the company and my colleagues, I could actually understand the president's choice and I believed that new opportunities would come up for which I would be tapped.

A few months later the president was replaced with another. The company agenda changed as our new president declared that he was going to bring our division into the "new" world with a strict emphasis on the Internet, as challenged by our chairman. I raised my hand and won a post on the new self-directed Internet team. I would report directly to this new president and lead our company's Internet sales efforts. This was all good. I would report to the president, have a challenging new learning curve and continue to make myself valuable to the industry. Certainly, being a leader in an Internet startup couldn't hurt my résumé and marketability.

CHANGE, CONSTANT CHANGE

I led the TV-Web convergence sales charge with very successful results in spite of utter chaos, draining and negative power struggles, and unrelenting change. Late in that first year a new senior vice president was brought in to oversee the improvement of the company's IT operations and tech-led consolidation efforts, as well as the TV stations' Web sites. So, there I was, no longer reporting directly to the president, out of important meetings that our new manager would now take alone, kingmaking for a new leader I didn't know, feeling hidden again after much of the grueling groundwork to success had been forged. He wasn't a bad guy; in fact I liked him. He was full of energy and smarts and he gave us the cohesion, direction and discipline that our team desperately needed in a leader. He was also very good to me when I presented my departure to him. We had a sandwich together on one of my last days and he enthusiastically shared a story about a recent meeting where the chairman of our company congratulated him on the Internet revenues. My stomach flipped as I asked him, "So the chairman thinks you've done all this in 4 months?" We both turned a bit red and kept on eating our sandwiches, barely missing a beat. The king gets the credit and I suppose protocol wouldn't call for him to give the chairman names, but this story made me even more certain that leaving was the absolute right thing for me to do at this time in my life. ■

To reiterate, think hard before taking action after not winning a promotion. Consider all sides and decide if you were treated fairly. If you believe you were treated unfairly, ask yourself if you can live with the new regime and if you can continue to learn and grow in the company, assuming you still respect the company. Take your time and consider your actions deeply. The right answers and opportunities will present themselves every time.

> *Think hard before taking action after not winning a promotion. Consider all sides and decide if you were treated fairly.*

A word on winning: Be gracious and inclusive as you step into your new spot. Your new constituency will be watching how you handle yourself during the takeover. They will be looking for clues and sizing you up from their points of view, and there will be gossip about you as notes are compared. Your beginning counts for communication, security and environment. You might be the leader, but even for you—especially for you—there is only one time to make a first, good impression.

It was helpful to me that in both cases of loss described earlier, the men who did become my boss came to me individually and told me they wanted me to stay on board and showed empathy with my disappointment. I'm not totally naïve, and I realize I was a needed entity, but the courtesy was noteworthy.

Try to give people a chance before you make general conclusions about a group that will impact people specifically. After one management change, I was asked repeatedly by the new leaders to rank the people in the order in which I would *fire* them. I was appalled and repeatedly refused. I asked why they weren't interested in knowing who the strongest people were, or who needed what training, or if they could come to meetings or go on sales calls to make their own assessments. I felt these people were looking for blood before promise and clearly this did nothing to create trust. They marked me as a lioness protecting her cubs and it was not a good situation.

QUESTIONS

- Are you able to be objective about promotions lost?

- Can you understand why your competitor won over you?

- What can you learn from the person who won the job?

- Would you have been happy working with the person you'd be reporting to?

- Are you able to lose with dignity even if you believe you were wronged?

- What can you learn from this experience?

- Which competencies or comfort zones do you need to work on?

- What are the steps you can take to ensure success the next time?

- Do you respect your company and do you believe you will have other opportunities there?

- How can you turn loss into an advantage?

- How can you improve your patience, or relish it, while you consider your options?

7 EGO, FEAR, AND COMPETITION

Ego, fear, and competition are three powerful, two-sided engines. They can move you to great heights or to low, lonely bottoms. If you take the time to contemplate the virtues and flaws of each, you might conclude that it is better to downplay these drivers in your life. A business environment will often stir these ingredients to the forefront as necessities for survival, if not achievement. With a little work you will understand the negative connotations better and be able to tweak them just enough to make some peace with these commonplace impulses.

Ego is a powerful force because it ostensibly pushes a person to win. Ego propels a person to be out in front, to have the spotlight, to be known as "the best" and to be the magnet at a meeting or a party. Ego and pride do not easily allow a person to fail or to seem weak in front of others. Ego can commandeer territorialism and lead to exclusive behavior. Ego can hurt others as the egotist dominates, controls and hoards information and contacts to keep the power position. Ego blinds you to the truth and robs you of the opportunity to see new roads to success. Ego could lead you to accept positions that you might ultimately dislike or not excel in, purely because of the title or the invitation and because ego can strip you of objectivity.

Ego leads some people to believe they are better than they are, more indispensable than is true and more possessive of complete knowledge. Ego can actually stunt growth because a person already believes he or she is big enough, smart enough, and has the requisite stamina and strategy to conquer anything. Ego can lead people to believe they are above all rules, and even above the law.

> *Ego leads some people to believe they are better than they are, more indispensable than is true and more possessive of complete knowledge.*

Ego can also be a huge drain on the people in the lives of the egoist, both at work and at home.

Ego is not the same as confidence. Confidence gives you the grounded ammunition you need to go for a promotion, submit new ideas, or disagree in a respectful way. Confidence helps you to make honest assessments about your competencies, goals and current environment. Confidence gives you the courage and grace to handle change within the organization or in your life in a way that is calm and measured without diluting enthusiasm and belief. Confidence helps you to navigate a minefield planted by a terrible boss, while ego might find you in a losing game of one-upmanship. Ego can propel action that is actually not positive for your life, while confidence is a conscious internal behavior gauge. Ego also causes disappointments to loom large in your mind, while confidence gives you the resilience to move forward.

Competition, in the positive view, creates an atmosphere of productivity and highly spirited traction. Competition from a capitalist viewpoint benefits the consumer through improved products, more choice and lower prices. Competition in the work world can also promote innovation and greater output of work. People who are motivated to grow and to lead are constantly looking for ways to stand out; they are achievers and winners. This is well and good so long as ego and fear aren't the main drivers and the true spirit of competition is manifested in work and action that benefits the greatest group and good.

Competition thrives in several work atmospheres. If you are in an ego-driven "divide and conquer" scenario, people will be pitted against each other and one team will lose. The leader is the winner because his or her agenda will be promoted and the personal feelings of the constituents are a second consideration to the personal win.

As a positive example, one competitive scheme might be an incentive sales contest where the company will win and so will the contestants. Even the team that doesn't achieve the prize will gain something because of the strategy, enthusiasm, creativity and fulfillment of the pursuit. The company wins through objectives reached, innovative ideas, and possibly new light shined on rising star talent from either team. The manner in which both teams are treated, after the contest is concluded, will make the emotional difference in the participant's take-away of the experience.

A different divide and conquer scheme occurs when the winner takes all and the loser loses everything. In one scenario, the general sales manager of a major television station left and his position was held open to accrue savings and to give the general manager time to decide who would replace him. The two local sales managers, each a serious contender for the position, divided the responsibilities of the sales department. Both worked very hard, overseeing hundreds of millions of dollars in revenue, while dealing with a demanding boss who they were each trying to impress, as well as ongoing personnel and process issues. They ran the sales department well through extreme pressure and after nearly a full year the general manager was replaced with another. The new GM learned of the situation and wanted to put an end to the nonsense and hire a general sales manager. After a year of competition to impress one manager, each candidate had one meeting with the new GM before he made his choice. One of them was promoted. The other was left to deal with extreme disappointment, embarrassment, astonishment, pity from the troops and customers, and ultimately chose to take a different job in the company.

Ego also causes disappointments to loom large in your mind, while confidence gives you the resilience to move forward.

Sometimes when two team leaders are given the same objectives, hurdles, and time to improve a situation, solve a problem, or meet a revenue target, ego, fear and competition can become propellers. In this sort of scheme, urgency and secrecy can take center stage and winning by drawing blood from the enemy seems to be the only acceptable result. Customers can unknowingly become part of the competition when both teams counter each other to close a sale. The people are left bruised and the company could find itself in an embarrassing situation. The company might have lost the respect and loyalty of the A player who doesn't value winning or losing this way. When ego and fear drive competition, you might have a sour taste regardless of the win. To some, winning a competition fueled by a personal ego or fear reaction is not as sweet as winning from a clean desire to just do great work.

Fear sometimes propels us to execute objectives with excellence because we don't want to fail. Fear sometimes makes us work harder and smarter so that we succeed. Fear can also promote action in a defensive way. A person in fear (survival) mode works to keep the status quo so that energy and focus can be spent surveying the terrain for the best ways to stay alive. Survival mode rips the ego and drains the brain of any creative or new thought because it is filled with obsession and plotting. Fear mode puts the mind's eye in the rearview mirror, or on the new leadership or other cause of change that is bringing about the fear. Fear is induced by insecurity and change, by a domineering or elusive manager, and by a perceived or real lack of support. A shaky economy and weak job market do not help either.

> *A person in fear (survival) mode works to keep the status quo so that energy and focus can be spent surveying the terrain for the best ways to stay alive.*

Fear for your job can be deepened and prolonged by lack of communication from the person above you. Ignorance can lead to fear and might create an atmosphere of negative fodder that only circulates that fear mode among a larger constituency. In other words, if your manager is in fright mode, chances are that he or she is more withdrawn than usual, is more nervous and snappish than usual, has moments of fire, but mostly retreats from subordinates at large. You might find that your manager tightens the reins and becomes more controlling. The effect of fearful management on a group can be devastating in the worst case, or create a laissez-faire atmosphere even in the best case. It is uncomfortable, stifling, unproductive and a clear waste of energy and time. Fear can paralyze you. The more afraid you are to take action, the less action you will take, until you are stuck in the hold of inertia. This slaps the ego and you could find yourself in a downward spiral that is difficult to dig out of.

Fearful people will either retreat and create an undoing for themselves or they will dig into the more positive parts of a balanced and confident persona to revive a competitive spirit and become resilient, creative and refocused. They will save themselves or destroy themselves as it relates to their work and the way they are able to personalize ego, fear and competition.

> *Fearful people will either retreat and create an undoing for themselves or they will dig into the more positive parts of a balanced and confident persona to revive a competitive spirit and become resilient, creative and refocused.*

Ego, fear, and competition, when not controlled, can lead to politics of the worst kind. People will become involved in territorial and power struggles that create barricades to communication and real drains on energy and productivity. When two high-level managers are engaged in a power war, their subordinates suffer because the managers are stressed and preoccupied beyond the day-to-day obligations, and energy is spent in the wrong place. Lines are drawn, designating whom the subordinate should speak or adhere to regardless of need.

If you are working on something that crosses over from your area to one under different leadership, discuss the matter with your manager and the other area leader before you proceed. Sell them on the merit of the project by showing the benefits to both areas. If either person you are approaching is known to be territorial, then don't be surprised or upset if he or she becomes a hurdle to your project, or wants to become a bigger part of it than you had hoped.

If you are aware of the personalities that surround and lead you, projecting their reactions will not be difficult. If you predict correctly and a storm ensues, try to be the calm in the storm. Chances are you were doing your job, or going above and beyond the normal thinking for your area. You probably deserve kudos for your idea from a larger company viewpoint, but if these people perceive that you are stepping on their power it will take them a while to gain that outlook, if they ever do. It doesn't move you forward to become upset by a reaction that you actually expect, so try to stop yourself from obsessing over conduct that you cannot control. If you have a great idea and it goes nowhere because of politics, copy high-level people on memos, or ask your manager to forward them with a copy to you, so there is an awareness of your thought processes and the idea itself. Sometimes an idea is just ahead of its time, but it is helpful to the organization and to you to get your efforts on the radar screen. The most important thing is that you do not stop innovating because of a blockhead manager. To stop initiating when you are a creative person is to let a part of you die; why would you give anyone the power to lessen the enjoyment and dignity of your spirit or your work?

> *The most important thing is that you do not stop innovating because of a blockhead manager. Expect and plan for the worst behaviors from those famous for delivering them.*

Expect and plan for the worst behaviors from those famous for delivering them. Try hard not to take it personally, explain yourself calmly, and let the higher-ups battle it out. Save yourself the grief and continue to contribute. If, over time, you feel the environment is blind to new thinking, or that you are not gaining for your offerings, you will have a whole different set of decisions to make.

If you are a higher-level executive and find yourself in these battles, take a look at your own activity. Are you territorial? Do you block innovation because of ego, fear or competition? These emotional drivers might be the culprits that bring you to negative (or no) action. Take a step back and ask yourself if you can enhance the company and your unit, even your own career, by joining forces with another group for the greater good of the company. In today's climate, businesses are looking for ways to leverage their strengths across a broader board. If you are a hindrance to that sort of progress in your company and you gain a reputation for it, you might rue the day that you first started to say "no" to innovation for purely personal power reasons. You would be the bigger winner if you listen to an idea objectively, decide on its merit, and help to champion the great ones. A cooperative leader beats a fighter every time and this doesn't mean always agreeing. It means being diplomatic in the course of action one takes, disagreeing for the right reasons, and not thwarting further creation and innovation.

> *Businesses are looking for ways to leverage strengths across a broader board. If you are a hindrance to that sort of progress in your company, you might rue the day that you first started to say "no" to innovation for purely personal power reasons.*

Ego, fear, and competition can motivate to great ends or they can each be toxins that threaten a person, place, group, division, and company. Ego, fear, and competition are loud bellwethers. Aware people would admit to living and working with these circumstances at one point or another in their career. If your ego starts to scream, try to take a deep breath and do your best to survey the situation from an objective point of view. Perhaps you feel slighted or invisible or not counted on in an important circumstance. An ego jolt could actually propel you to take action and defend a position that you believe in, or gain a better understanding about the perceptions of you and your work. You can cancel the fear mode by concentrating on the integrity of excellent work, through which you gain free agency, and having your own long-term personal freedom (financial) plan. If you are working for someone in the fear mode, you can either retreat by staying under the radar screen until the problem is solved, or you can actually excel by moving forward and helping with the problem. If you are able to shun fear you will be able to continue to innovate and to promote a healthy and positive atmosphere of results and productivity around you.

Ego and competition drive action. Ego is harmful when it overtakes truth and blinds you from further learning and making sound decisions, or if it leads you to underestimate others, including the competition. Feeling jealous about someone else's promotion or growth, even if you didn't want the job, is not unusual, and it is a manifestation of ego and competition. Letting go of ego isn't easy, but doing so will save you some angst and internal negative speak.

Competition hurts us when ego and fear are mixed together to drive someone to "assault and kill" anyone on the way to a win. Competition, be it internal or external, can be appreciated and tackled in a constructive way. Acknowledging your competition helps you understand the hurdles you face on your way to success. Although it is helpful to your cause to declare who your chief rivals are, you could argue that to regard the competition as the enemy is a bit hyperbolic. Your main competitors have reached that status because they are doing something right, after all. To call the competition stupid or worse magnifies the ignorance and myopia of the leader who believes it. Historical losses in war were caused in part by discounting the enemy.

Acknowledging your competition helps you understand the hurdles you face on your way to success.

Do you agree that it is better to view your competitor's actions based on their objectives, people resources, current market share and product positioning? By understanding their position and challenges in the larger scheme, you can understand their advantages and disadvantages and begin to predict their strategies. If you respect and understand your competition enough to project their actions, you are in a better place to win. Knowing the competition's strengths and flaws will help you to find your own competitive niche. The marketer who disparages the competition, beyond provable facts, runs the risk of alienation and being marked as arrogant by their customers.

There is room for more than one company in a category to achieve growth, and this actually serves our market economy best. The goal at most major companies is to dominate their market; in its most measurable form this means a real commitment to quality, customers, and human resources, as well as profit.

Ego, fear, and competition are each two-sided. Be aware so that you can use them to your benefit. Together, these three elements can be overwhelming if they surround you in a negative fashion. If you find yourself in an environment where these attributes are out front, you might begin to feel that you are in an unhealthy space. If you are caught in a negative funnel you might find that you are more competitive than you'd like, more driven by ego than you are proud to admit, and more aware of fear as a spirit killer than you ever knew possible. Ego, fear and competition are not always peaceful but they are almost always a force of action.

> *The goal at most major companies is to dominate their market; in its most measurable form this means a real commitment to quality, customers, and human resources, as well as profit.*

QUESTIONS

- Do you have a healthy ego?

- Which ego-based career decisions have you made?

- Are you happy with the outcome?

- Does your ego blind you to truths about your competencies?

- How can you work on your confidence level so that it overrides your ego?

- Do ego, fear, and competition drive you to hoard knowledge or contacts?

- What makes you fearful in the work world?

- How can fear propel you positively?

- What steps can you take to harness fear?

- How can you use your fear to preempt survival mode?

- Might you work for a competitor one day?

- Are you a healthy competitor? Must you go for blood, or do a competent analysis and a cogent strategy help you get to the win?

8 THE RESPONSIBILITY OF LEADERSHIP

Here are a couple of sayings you might have heard: "The fish stinks from the head" and "Not to each other." These aren't lines from a television screenplay for an episode of *The Sopranos*. They are axioms for the importance of leadership to the feel, progress and viability of an organization. "Not to each other" means not to lie or fool one another, that trust is integral to the organization and the way in which leaders lead makes all the difference to productivity, truth and the honor of great work.

Leadership qualities include integrity, passion, credibility, vision, courage, product and sector knowledge, the ability to articulate the vision, decisiveness, accountability, empathy, inclusion, positive mental attitude, charisma, and the ability to attract and retain key players to the organization.

I had the good fortune to work for GE/NBC when Jack Welch was the chairman. He was an absolute dynamo who had passion, vision, knowledge, the charisma to rally a rock and little tolerance for fools. He pushed his agendas fearlessly and with blinders on. The company leader's were driven to innovate, dare and stretch, to be the number one or two company in each sector, to challenge the employee base to meet and exceed competencies, and to manage the weak and the lazy out. Mr. Welch visited the field twice a year to get to know who the emerging leaders were. He questioned us mercilessly, and we were aware that he had the answers and we'd better have them, too. Jack Welch was an exceptionally strong chairman, to the benefit of the company and its stockholders.

A person is identified as a leader, in part, if he or she is able to motivate people to actions that will benefit the company, the team and the individual for the long-term. Motivating people to greater action than they believe possible comes from passion and the ability to articulate vision in a way that is clear, inclusive and begs no credibility questions. The enlightened leader cares about the environment so that productivity thrives and customer relations are a top priority over bureaucracy and politics. The goal of the place is bigger than any one person; fulfillment, passion, exuberance, and profit will follow naturally as a result of this diligence.

> *The enlightened leader cares about the environment so that productivity thrives and customer relations are a top priority over bureaucracy and politics.*

Leaders who act and work in an ethical manner draw trust from the working body and build a sense of safety as well. Today's leaders must emphasize truth in financial reporting and develop communications so that credibility is transparent throughout the organization. Legislated or not, credibility structures, such as the Sarbanes-Oxley Act, need to be woven into daily behavior once again and across the board.

Leadership qualities and actions are not dependent on a job description or title, and it is important to grasp these characteristics whether you are a manager, executive or an aspirant to one of these posts, and to exhibit them with regularity.

Attracting and retaining key employees is crucial for many reasons; replacement costs are an expensive proposition for a company on many levels. Losing a strong player is especially risky in the current world of headcount reductions, because you cannot be sure that the job will be replaced, or the post might be held open longer than usual to accrue savings. Burn out on the part of stressed employees who are asked to cover could also create more defections and yet another job to be filled. Being smart about the people you hire and protecting the environment has never been more vital.

Being decisive, especially under pressure, is an integral leadership quality because the defining actions notify your working body about policy, strategy and clarity of vision toward the future. As a decisive leader, you will also lend a sense of security to the employee base because action is almost always better than ambivalence. Being fair yet firm compels integrity, accountability, empathy, trust and respect from both the leader and the led.

As leaders, you have the responsibility of creating environments that lead to success for the company and the individuals who work with and for you. Communicative and inclusive behavior on your part exhibits trust, respect and expectations for the team. An open-door policy and encompassing setting assures that each person is important to the mission, and might motivate everyone on your team to do more. Asking key employees for input on strategy and process puts them in the middle of the action and helps to promote a personal investment in the cause.

Building environments that encourage employees to safely speak out invites innovation and daring, and could also lead to cost savings through the admission of errors or recommendations for process enhancements. Learning what doesn't work well, from the source of the work, goes a long way toward keeping an area productive *and* profitable. Don't you enjoy believing that you make a difference in the workplace? The more that you encourage people to contribute the more they will. This will add to your growth benefit and to the company's success.

> *Building environments that encourage employees to safely speak out invites innovation and daring, and could also lead to cost savings through the admission of errors or recommendations for process enhancements.*

Take, for instance, the case of Jim Despain. He started working for Caterpillar as a night janitor, sweeping the halls.

He held several positions during his many years with the company before becoming a divisional vice president, and his insight into all the levels made him consider the need for empowerment of all 3,000 of the company's employees.[1] His respect for every worker made him aware of the need for dignity and self-worth at every level. His approach to leadership was considered fresh and innovative. But was it? Or was it the fundamental common sense principle of treating others as you wish to be treated?

As a hiring manager, you must posses a clear understanding of the business strategies and objectives, and the job stress level, to create comprehensive competency criteria for each open job. The interview is a research process to unveil the matching characteristics between the candidate and the current company need. The required abilities change as the shape of the team and business needs change, so staying abreast of the whole picture of the business unit is imperative.

Integrity and empathy go a long way to inform and shape an environment and to retain employees. Integrity by example leads the employee population to work and act a way that is ethical and trustworthy. Empathic leadership opens the doors for information from the working body that can strengthen the place and allow for greater understanding of what motivates each person. Empathy will help you motivate each person from the position of his or her emotional drivers and broaden stakeholder consensus and trust. Insight into a person's trigger points will also help you understand each person's reward system and assist in conflict resolution.

> *Empathic leadership opens the doors for information that can strengthen the place and allow for greater understanding of what motivates each person.*

Companies win loyalty when they actually change policies to reflect their employees' needs and desires. You will find many creative ways that companies use to retain their valued

---

1. Jane Bodman Converse and James E. Despain. *And Dignity for All: Unlocking Greatness with Values-Based Leadership* (Upper Saddle River, NJ: Financial Times Prentice Hall, 2003).

employees in *Fortune* magazine's annual survey of the 100 Best Companies to Work For.[2] A few examples follow here and include second-ranked Pfizer. Rather than cutting benefits in a tough year, Pfizer actually expanded them. Employees now receive three weeks of vacation after one year of service; previously they had to wait five years. The company also increased its adoption aid benefit from $5,000 to $10,000 and began offering a vision plan as part of its health insurance coverage.

Despite Wall Street woes, Goldman Sachs, ranked 35th, said it maintained all its benefits in 2003, including a $5,000 contribution to every employee's 401(k) plan. Plus, it recently added vision coverage to the health insurance policy.

J.M. Family Enterprises, a Deerfield Beach, Florida, Toyota distributor, ranked 14th, added more perks to its already lavish list of benefits, including an on-site hair salon, a medical clinic with two physicians, a lap pool and recognition cruises on a company yacht. In 2002, J.M. Family Enterprises opened an on-site child-care center and began offering retirees with 10 years' service a health insurance plan in which the premium is split 50-50.

These companies, and the other 97 on *Fortune*'s list, believe that protecting the employee base also protects their long-term interests. These companies made the list because their employees voted for them. As one employee from a listed company said, "There is a sense that we sink or swim as one big family." Environments do matter to output and perspective.

Environments do matter to output and perspective.

Mistakes should be fixed promptly and with little alarm so that people will continue to innovate. Are you more or less likely to report a mistake when fear and intimidation rule the day? The (costly) problem could go on longer than necessary if you are reluctant to speak up. As the leader, learn from the mistake rather than solely admonish for it. A mistake can be an opportunity to create new processes and encourage ideas

2. Robert Levering and Milton Moskowitz. "100 Best Companies to Work For 2003," *Fortune.* © FORTUNE 2003, Time, Inc. All rights reserved.

that will change and grow the organization positively. An error could also shine light on the need for more training or an employee's weaknesses that need to be addressed. When a person who has integrity makes an error of some magnitude, he or she will feel terrible about the situation and be his or her own worst admonisher. You can fix the problem without the added necessity of public blame and move on.

Finally, there is the matter of legacy when it comes to responsible leadership. What will your imprint be long after you've left? Your actions as a leader teach by example and have a great deal of impact on the surrounding employees for years into the future. The examples you set can help to determine the actions of the whole next crop of leadership. The environment that your leadership promotes is an important legacy, as are the openness to talent, innovation, creativity, increased productivity, commitment to results, grace under extreme pressure, and communication, to name only a few components.

Mentoring talented people to grow within your organization and industry is key to the future and to your own legacy. Helping a strong talent to become a kingmaker within the company while respecting his or her whole life is a great goal within the larger scheme of things.

QUESTIONS

- How do you fare against the list of leadership competencies listed in this chapter?

- How can you exhibit these behaviors in your current position?

- How important is it to you that your thoughts on policy decisions matter?

- What competencies do you most respect in your current business leadership?

- What type of environment do you enjoy and thrive in most and how can you promote it?

- Do you handle mistakes as opportunities or major problems?

- Do you have empathy for your colleagues and managers?

- What will your legacy be?

9 THE CHAMPION

The importance of a champion, or supermentor, to your career cannot be stressed enough. I had a few great bosses with whom I shared a thriving work relationship, and I even learned much from those whose behavior didn't inspire me. I never had one long-standing champion, though, and I think

> If I could change one thing from the past this would be it.

that made the road to some promotions tougher for me. I switched companies four times over 24 years and I was also a bit reticent when it came to cultivating this type of alliance. If I could change one thing from the past this would be it. It is a serious lesson that I hope you will listen to. If you hope to have a long career in one place or one industry it is not enough to only earn the trust and respect of the people that matter in the company. You must also let high-level management know you beyond the business shell so that a real bonding and comfort zone can develop. Comfort and trust come with time and exposure.

We had several criteria for hiring when we opened a national rep firm. Along with product knowledge, negotiation skills, and contacts, we wanted to hire people that we'd invite to our homes for dinner. We wanted our people to be a bright spot in a customer's hectic day. The people who represented our stations would be solution oriented *and* enjoyable to be with. This same principle holds true for your internal customers. When everyone is stressed, time spent around people who are productive, positive, and fun makes the day easier and more enjoyable.

Style and social compatibility between you and the hiring manager gives you an edge over competition that doesn't have it. Compatibility and comfort grows as you learn the working style of those you report to and adapt to their way of doing business. Hopefully, your manager will also work to identify your motivators so that you will come together for the greater good. Self-promotion is not comfortable to many people; gaining a champion who will do this for you is a more efficient, comfortable, and durable route in the long run.

Champions are people who have clout in an organization due to historical success. Champions are also likely to be generous leaders because they have the freedom, experience and confidence to teach. Well-placed generosity framed in avocation costs nothing and gains them plenty. They understand their power and use it to push their agendas, and people are a big part of the cards they play. It is gratifying and significant for them to look around and see the people who are on a fast career track partly because of their input. That's okay, because the winners abound. The winners include you, the company, your customers, and ultimately the champions in the first place. The great champions have across-the-board influence that they appreciate but don't abuse.

> *Champions are people who have clout in an organization due to historical success.*

Identify a leader with champion potential and begin to build toward a relationship with this person. Let your direct manager know that you are interested in this prominent person as a high-level champion. Stress that this will not usurp his or her authority over you; in fact, your interest might augment the manager's position to this champion. Offer to report back to your manager on any meetings you have with the champion. Perhaps your direct manager could even open the door for you with a phone call or in-person conversation with the champion-mentor.

If your immediate manager does not like the idea, try to engage him or her in conversation so that you can understand the reasons (maybe your boss is without a champion, or feels threatened). If the answer remains negative, it is not a good idea to go over your boss's head and move forward with the idea just then. Another route is to write a memo to your HR department or to the president of the division or company suggesting high-level leaders be matched with high-potential employees to give those employees wider knowledge and exposure. Your idea might be a welcome solution for company leaders who want to know the talent pool better, and your manager might gain in the bargain. Assuming you have approval, ask for occasional guidance from the champion in the form of informational interviews on an infrequent, but regular, basis. In most cases the champion will be flattered and happy to help. You've probably met this person before, and your manager has hopefully introduced your idea, so the first meeting will not be a totally cold call. Ask for time and begin by directly expressing what your interest is, that you respect this person as a company influencer, that you would like to get to know each other better and learn from him or her. Present what you bring to the organization as a person and a professional as well.

> *Suggest high-level leaders be matched with high-potential employees to give those employees wider knowledge and exposure.*

The first meeting could be light, covering your background, résumé, and your interests and career goals. Sprinkle in enough of the champion's background and the key (work-related) reasons that helped you identify him or her as someone you would like to learn and otherwise benefit from. Preparation for ensuing meetings should be ongoing. Keep a "champion file" with examples of your good work, visions and ideas for the future, and suggestions to improve the workplace. Keep a subfile of questions for discussion, which could include political, ethical, industry, and company environment issues. You might not hit on every topic in your meetings, but your preparedness will show that you are eager to learn, have something to offer, and respect time pressures, too.

You have nothing to lose by asking for these meetings if you are a true contributor with competencies that the company and this champion will find attractive. You have much to gain through the exposure and by becoming a lieutenant to a key leader.

> *Learn as much as possible from this person and volunteer to work on special projects that he or she might be spearheading.*

Learn as much as possible from this person and volunteer to work on special projects that he or she might be spearheading. Be reliable, passionate, open, and trustworthy and you might gain a person who believes in you and supports and advocates your growth. Your value is in your hard work, creativity, contribution, and future potential. The champion's value is in a treasure trove of knowledge, life and work experience, and contacts to be shared.

If you are in a satellite office, your manager at headquarters becomes your main conduit to the company's wider knowledge about your work, integrity, and style. Exposure and gaining mentorship from a remote location presents its own set of challenges. Your work will speak first in this instance. It is important to take the time for extra preparedness so that you will become a valuable contributor on conference call meetings. Volunteer to be a presenter at in-person conferences and to be part of company-wide initiatives that are the hot new thing. Take advantage of social events when you are at headquarters or when upper management is at your location. Plan ahead for a meeting or a meal, or a meeting over a meal if you can.

Visiting a home office can have its own set of minefields. You want to develop relationships with the people in your company that you don't see every day without overstepping. At the same time, you want your work to count as much as the headquarters natives. For example, you work in Columbus, Ohio, and your headquarters is in New York. You come in for a meeting and you have a presentation slot on the agenda. You want to impress your New York colleagues, and although you don't feel lesser than them, you might put more pressure on yourself to impress than you need to. Just be prepared, friendly, and confident in your message and value and get on with the show. For all you know, the home office person envies your remote location, a bit off the radar screen perhaps, but also away from the thick politics of his or her day-to-day routine. You can lead and prove your value to an organization from any location.

You could argue that there is no such thing as altruism because, even as a champion, people get back what they give. The agenda is secondary because the fact is that you need to be sponsored by someone who is very smart, generous, interested in mentoring, and respected in the company and the industry. It will never hurt you to have a boss or mentor who has a strong, respected voice in the company. Your responsibility and charge is to mentor the next generation in kind.

Developing talent in promising people is a great source of fulfillment and I encourage you to take this responsibility as a true purpose and as an expansion of what you bring to the company. Mentoring is a keen reflection on your leadership skills and business philosophies. Working closely with people to grow them into company influencers helps to propagate the core values you hold dear. This is good for your organization and it is true legacy building as well. Mentoring and championing is a great bargain for all.

QUESTIONS

- Do you have a champion?

- Who do you identify as the key leaders that you could learn from?

- How comfortable are you in building relationships with people outside of your zone?

- How comfortable are you with asking for a champion?

- What can you do to become more comfortable pursuing a champion? (Discussion with your direct manager to set up periodic interviews? Suggest the idea to Human Resources?)

- Can you identify comfort and style issues as a stumbling block to promotion in your own career?

- Do you seek out employees with strong potential to develop and mentor?

10 EMBRACE DIVERSITY

The drive toward diversity among our workforce continues, yet some still confuse diversity with affirmative action. It can be confusing. To many people, diversity represents forced integration, even in this day and age. The fact that our own local communities reflect a global sort of multiculturalism through immigration, education, and skilled competencies escapes many.

Affirmative action came into play as a tool to help people from cultures different from the current workplace majority break into areas of work and life where they had not been before. In some cases, quotas reflecting an area's demographics are derived as a guide to employer headcount objectives. Although diversity can be argued as an honorable charge, it is not easily delivered if the outreach from a corporation is not pointed in this direction as a clear objective. Why?

> *Diversity is not easily delivered if the outreach from a corporation is not pointed in this direction as a clear objective.*

- People like to hire and work with people who look, act, believe, and think as they do because it's more comfortable and you can get from point A to point B faster when everyone understands each other with ease.

- Potential candidates might not be aware of or feel welcome to apply for opportunities within your industry. Targeted recruitment is essential to introduce your company to a new field of candidates.

- The people already in place might not have the interest, the will, or the social or business contacts that could lead to the hiring of capable, diverse employees.

- Hiring managers fear litigation, under the cloak of discrimination, even if an employee is in breach with cause.

Diversity means differences or variety in culture and belief systems. Two merits of bringing people of different cultures into a new corporate zone are in the opportunity for innovation and a better understanding of multicultural consumer predilections. Another reason for including and embracing people from minority groups is simply that our population is changing. The workforce needs to reflect this change to keep people skilled and growing, and for companies to have the ability to replace the current workforce with the next generation of workers. That next generation will not look exactly like the one we're in now, and it is up to us to get them ready. In fact, Deloitte & Touche, a professional services firm, estimates from 2000 U.S. census data that by 2010, nearly 70 percent of new entrants into the workforce will be women and people of color.[1]

Deloittte & Touche and a few companies so enlightened are taking diversity a step beyond the obvious race and gender codes. Deloitte & Touche's Jim Wall, national managing director of human resources, explains it this way: "We serve people globally, and we do that with people. In order to serve our clients with excellence, we need the very best people, not the very best that fit into two or three buckets. We talk about things like value systems, language, geographic experience and location, working style, thinking style, educational background, involvement in the military, socioeconomic class, religion—all the things that make up the dynamics of who we are."

---

1. Molly Rose Teuke. "Rethinking Diversity." *Continental Airline Magazine* (March 2003).

Diversity is a vehicle whereby people bring different life and cultural experiences to the company that can expand vision, increase innovation, stir environments, create positive competition, and improve the workplace.

What can a room full of upper crust, well-connected, White suburban adults know well about reaching teens with a sparkly nail polish or a Hispanic audience when introducing a new car or getting on the wavelength of a young urban male to market cool jeans? Yes, they can acquire research to guide the marketing and manufacturing decisions, but anecdotal information from people who come from the consumer's place is also invaluable.

It is not enough to hire a diverse workforce to fill a quota sheet or to comply with equal opportunity laws. This does no good for the person or the company; competency standards must be held in force and the value of this new and different employee must be respected and acknowledged. A person from a non-majority group needs to be mentored, championed, and developed so that his or her assimilation will occur swiftly in spite of real and perceived differences.

One difficult part of the reckoning is in the acknowledgment and needed belief that a diverse workforce is better for the company and for the people who will mentor them.

The benefit of a diverse workforce is not easily sold because some hiring and employee practices have not held to the belief that excellence is the first key to success and excellence has no color, gender, race, or ethnicity. The measure of quality and contribution has to be the same for all people in the work population so that groups are not segmented and stereotypes can be broken. Expectations will move people to stretch to greater heights and the stretch should be shared equally. The company and the minority person will shift from a "we/they" to an "us" society and questions of tokenism will drop only when excellent work cancels doubt.

> *The benefit of a diverse workforce is not easily sold because some hiring and employee practices have not held to the belief that excellence has no color, gender, race, or ethnicity.*

It takes time for a new group to break through walls of doubt. I started selling television advertising time in 1977 when women in this particular workforce were still rare; we were the new minority group. It was not an easy road for my few female colleagues and me. We suffered sexual harassment and serious pay discrepancies, and we had to fight for key clients because most of the buying constituency were female and our managers believed men could get a better market share from them than we could.

We worked very hard and leaned on each other and charged, through consistently excellent work, that we be taken seriously. We pitched jobs that we didn't get over and over again, but we didn't stop pitching and we finally got them. We were told to go for the lesser jobs in the least important markets, but we competed for the top jobs in the biggest markets. We thrust ourselves and our values, ideas, and work ethics into everything we did. It took a long time, and although women still do not prevail, we are no longer thought to be in need of affirmative action because we are now part of the norm. Sexual harassment is now punishable, pay discrepancies have lessened, women are real competition for key positions, and efforts at work–life balance have made spouses more equal in relieving outside pressures.

It was not immediately comfortable for many leaders to champion women, the new minority in the workforce at the time. That action required some courage and belief in the competencies of the person, the ideal of meritocracy, and an identified company objective to include and promote this group. The real challenge and opportunity beyond hiring minorities is in the mentoring and training of these individuals. Without the benefit of deep product knowledge, process intelligence, cultural wisdom, and contacts in place, the new (minority) employee needs a person to lean on, learn from, and be accountable to.

> *To embrace diversity means to break stereotypes and to lead and act in ways that bring separating walls down.*

To thrive in his or her career a minority person needs a champion even more than the majority person because many hiring leaders are less likely to be comfortable with someone from a different culture. Although this sort of discomfort can be chalked up to human nature, it is the above-the-norm effort of mentoring that will create change and acceptance. When the mentor gets to know and believe in the protege, the acceptance within the company will grow.

To embrace diversity means to break stereotypes and to lead and act in ways that bring separating walls down. It might mean facing your own prejudices and predispositions so that you can open your mind enough to gain an understanding of the talent this new person possesses as well as the obstacles he or she might face that are different from your own. When you become inclusive through mentorship you will gain the opportunity for new learning and expansion of your own experience as a leader and a human.

Embracing diversity also means having the courage to discuss the general rules of conduct about appropriate attitude and behavior in a way that is helpful, nonthreatening, and nonjudgmental. This sort of advice will help the new person realize ways in which they can better fit and prosper in a specific environment even beyond the expectation of great work. Discussions of attitude might revolve around the company culture and its mission statement or charter. These documents were written for all employees equally, the expectations are the same for all, and they should be discussed with all. An attitude that highlights product knowledge, team play, open communication, process and time management, a sense of urgency, customer relations, manufacturing excellence, leadership by example, accountability, and a willingness to stretch are some examples of workplace guidelines. Hearing this information from the human resource department is one thing. Gaining this information through a mentor's word and deed might have a different, more personal resonance for the new employee.

> *We have become so politically correct that we are sometimes uneven and insufficient in our leadership.*

Behavior issues can seem more delicate and include such "givens" as being on time, not missing work, appropriate language and dress, conduct at meetings or social-business events, and so on. We have become so politically correct that we are sometimes uneven and insufficient in our leadership. Help the new person assimilate more quickly by conveying the acceptable protocols of the place. This sort of discussion can be handled diplomatically and doesn't have to cause a problem. For example, I remember in the late 1980s advising female salespeople, then a minority, that they must wear panty hose, even in the 95-degree, humid dog days of a New York summer. This conversation was very uncomfortable for me, but we wanted to present ourselves professionally to our internal and external customers, and bare legs would not help to advance our cause.

Advising a person to dress the part or use appropriate language is no different than teaching someone which fork to use in a restaurant. It doesn't change the core of what makes them special, it just helps them to become more easily assimilated, less different, and more a part of the work culture they are in. Blending into a new environment does not mean abdicating culture; culture is precious, beautiful, and important. Understanding the internal audience and appealing to style comfort zones is simply a smart way to go for every employee.

The responsibility of the minority hire to embrace and strive for excellence is everything. Nothing trumps stereotypes like actions that reflect the opposite of the stereotype. If you are a minority (or any new) hire, there are steps you can take to begin your road to success. Ask your manager or HR person for a copy of the annual review that you will be judged against a year from your hire. Study the competencies you will be measured against so that you can see what matters to the company and strive to master them. Ask your manager who he or she perceives to be the strongest players on the team and observe these people in their day-to-day activity. If you agree that they are worthy of emulation ask if you can work closely with the A player of your choosing.

> *The responsibility of the minority hire to embrace and strive for excellence is everything. Nothing trumps stereotypes like actions that reflect the opposite of the stereotype.*

The gold mine is in the great opportunity and gateway for the person and the group he or she represents. It is fine to become friendly with people in the workforce who are more like you than not; it is not all right to form a we–they stronghold that keeps you separate or creates a reverse inclusive field. Good advice to people from a new diversity group is to apply yourself to every area of learning and exhibit a cooperative and tenacious attitude through a strong work ethic. Excellence and willingness override stereotypes every time.

The inclusion of competent minorities will benefit the employee base, create attraction from more people in new groups, and, in the long run, create competition that is healthier than cronyism for promotion. When you are open to learning from people whose cultures are different from our own, your own world will open up. Here again, you can see a real gain in giving because mentors learn, too.

Diversity in concert with accountability is a real plus for everyone. In a best-case scenario, opportunities open for a new group of people and new information and ideas are injected into the current culture. New or improved products come to market, companies grow market share and profits, consumers benefit from the new or improved products, and increased competition might yield lower prices.

Embrace diversity, not as a means to filling a quota card, but as a means to higher standards in ideas, creativity, and competition. What you gain about your world will manifest itself in heightened tolerance and personal growth.

QUESTIONS

- What prejudices or stereotypes do you hold?

- What stops you from wanting to hire a minority person?

- What can you change about the current role of development and mentorship for the minority hire?

- What advice would you give to the minority hire to speed acceptance and break stereotypes?

- Does your leadership hold the same standards of excellence for all hires?

- Can you identify a person you could mentor?

- What will you personally gain by embracing diversity?

- Are you curious about different cultures?

- Do you believe people are more alike than they are different?

- Do you believe that excellence has no color, religious affiliation, or sexual bias?

- What can you do to equalize your workplace?

- As a minority, what can you do to break doubt?

- As a minority, how can you shift from we–they to us, if this exists in your workplace?

SUMMARY OF PART I: PEOPLE, PROFIT, POLITICS, AND PROCESS

- A balanced and centered approach to your career begins with self-awareness while you measure your reactions to change and professional growth.
- Put yourself into thrive vs. survive mode by making excellence your security ticket. Be the one your company wants to keep and the competition wants to steal away. Be the "wow" hire.
- Being a kingmaker is a way to solidify your value to the organization, to your management, and to your own sense of free agency and security.
- With headcount reductions and each job counting for two, only the excellent employee will thrive. We could be headed for the ultimate meritocracy, as each post is weightier than ever.
- Profit is a chief goal of every corporation. Understanding this driver will help you to find fulfillment within the overriding goal. Contribution to growth and profit will enhance your value within the organization.
- It is imperative that people who matter know you as a person and a professional. Comfort zones matter as much or more than competency to some hiring managers.
- Practice ways to bring your comfort level up around the leaders in the organization without changing the core values that define you.

- Make the work your purpose over the politics so that you can direct energy and focus in a positive way. The honor of great work is a dignified objective and it will keep you from harm.

- Be aware of the true "agenda." Don't be afraid to ask for clarification.

- The way you lose is as important as the way you win promotions. Be gracious and take the time to reflect and learn from the episode. Think beyond the obvious before making any moves that you can't take back.

- Take the time you need in each post to learn as much as possible before moving on. Don't Peter Principle yourself. Be aware of what you want and why you want it.

- Handle change from a leadership position: Don't contribute to gossip, and help to clarify truth and direction. Embrace new direction or management with a positive mental attitude: innocent until proven guilty.

- Get comfortable with ego, fear, and competition: How do you manifest each? How can you improve and what can you let go of? How will getting a grip on these emotions make your life and career easier?

- Lead through empathy, clarity, focus, and positive energy. Keep your mind's eye on legacy.

- Identify people who are champion material and ask for mentorship. This is an imperative.

- Embrace diversity as a conduit to productivity, creativity, and innovation, as well as a way to bridge gaps in your own communities.

- Excellence has no gender, color, or religion. Excellence trumps stereotypes. Be accountable as the hiring manager or the diverse employee and open a gateway to your industry for a whole variety of people.

PART

EXCEL, EXECUTE, ENJOY!

KINGMAKER

11 VALUE YOURSELF IF YOU INTEND TO BE VALUABLE

Value is the assigned measure of worth that you appropriate to a subject, be it an idea, product, person, animal, or any other item you encounter. Value is largely intangible and in the eye and mind of the beholder. Something that is valuable to one might mean nothing to another. What is valuable to a company is one thing; what is valuable to you as a whole being might be something completely different. Values are flexible as priorities change over time, as you mature and learn from experience, and in response to people and events over which you have no control. In a solid economy where the workplace feels safe, you are more likely to take risks and be more willing to apply yourself with real passion and enthusiasm. When times are tough, when the world is not at peace, and when the economy suffers, you will have a different set of challenges to consider. In tough times when growth is not always a given and jobs do not feel secure you might witness, and be part of, actions, decisions, and environments that are new, wildly open-ended, and not in sync with your ethics or values. It is when jobs are not secure that you are more likely to see the dog-eat-dog, winner-take-all, survival-of-the-fittest, backstabbing parts of people's character.

It is important to take full measure of the climate that affects your workplace to discover how you must adapt to flourish rather than fear, thrive rather than merely survive, and stay true to yourself even if those around you don't.

This is fear and survival mode in live action, and it might cause real problems for you. It is important to take full measure of the climate that affects your workplace to discover how you must adapt to flourish rather than fear, thrive rather than merely survive, and stay true to yourself even if those around you don't.

Actions change over time in reaction to realities. Core personal values don't change, but the order of valuable priorities might be thrown topsy-turvy for a while, until complex situations are smoothed out. The hard part is to keep your values alive by not succumbing to harmful or deceitful tactics to survive. The goal is to remain true to your values while you are aware of changing ones in the workplace and while others cope in their own way. This might mean you have to be a bit more aggressive and aware to keep your place, but it doesn't mean you have to change the core of who you are. You can learn a lot in tough times. You learn which leaders and colleagues you respect most, who your real friends are, who has values in common with yours, and why the tough decisions about headcount or consolidation have to be made sometimes. You can also use a difficult time to develop your own leadership skills as you help colleagues push down their fear and choose the high road in conduct and contribution. In every case, the more the two value measures match the more likely you are to feel fulfilled and exuberant in the workplace. You can know real satisfaction in a corporate environment and you can do this in good times and in bad.

You can learn a lot in tough times. You learn which leaders and colleagues you respect most, who your real friends are, who has values in common with yours, and why the tough decisions about headcount or consolidation have to be made sometimes.

How can you hold on to yourself and continue to grow your value no matter the pressure context? You can start by understanding what makes your soul sing. What are the values you hold dear? What are the values your company stands for? How in sync are the two? How can your work add value to your company and to your life? How can your values and beliefs add value to the company? If you value yourself you are more likely to be valuable to an organization because you are more likely to have a personal quality stake in your work.

Personal values that you bring to your working life might include integrity, a sense of community, respect, attribution, contribution, creativity, stretch, opportunity, tolerance, trustworthiness, productivity, competitiveness, will, maturity, and a desire for fair market compensation (or better).

Company values might include integrity in good times and bad, open and honest communication especially in times of change, respect for human resources, best-practice sharing, and assimilating a very bright body of diverse employees. Company leadership will value people who are contributing, self-starting individuals, quick studies, and not averse to change. People with positive mental attitudes, who have an inspiring and motivating effect on their peer group, a healthy yet harnessed ambition and a sense of passion as they integrate honor and dignity into their work, are attractive to organizations. Why wouldn't they be? People that possess these values *make things happen* for the company, their customers, families, and themselves. The very independence involved in understanding your value set makes you enticing because you clearly know what you have to offer and what will make you happy. The understanding of what you bring to the party will also give you confidence, over ego, to help you make the right decisions along the way. People with these attributes have a passion for seeing the abstract turn into the concrete as quickly as possible.

It is important to think about your long-term life and career goals as you assess your values. Do you think that you'd like to be involved in your current industry for the rest of your working life? What else interests you? Might you see a dual or triple career journey in your lifetime? Are you able to incorporate your passions into your life, through your work or other outlets? How long do you want your working life to last? Do you see retirement at age 50 or 60 or 75 or 82? Do you think you will want a career switch at 45? It takes planning to make your choices a reality and it is never too early to have your goals in mind so that you can begin to take the appropriate actions toward them. How can becoming more valuable to an organization serve your long-term plans and purpose?

Hold your head high and work hard and smart. Learn, ask, absorb, and do. What is the next big thing in your company and industry and how can you become involved with it? What is keeping your CEO up at night? Are you able to make suggestions for practices or strategies that might prove to be a significant game changer? Attach yourself to the projects, people, and areas that matter most to the company. These will be easy to identify as you actively listen in meetings, gain an understanding of business and sector trends, and clearly comprehend where your company is headed. Ask for plum assignments that offer learning, new viewpoints, and exposure. Let your manager know of your interests and why you would be a key asset to that group and objective.

> *You must own your responsibility to your career and the work itself because it delivers your purpose, paycheck, branding, and future plans.*

Deliver complete work because your name is on it and your future rides on your performance. You must own your responsibility to your career and the work itself because, although this serves the company, it also delivers your purpose, paycheck, branding, and future plans. It also informs your sense of fulfillment and overall growth.

Comparing your values and skill sets with those of the company will help you see what you uniquely bring to the place. How will you make a difference? What gaps on the team will you fill? How will your energy and enthusiasm ignite the actions of others? How will you lead your peer group through change? How important is your very will to the actual goal delivery? How tolerant are you? Treat others as you want to be treated, and don't be afraid to set limits on how you expect to be treated.

The idea of setting boundaries on how you'd like to be treated might lead you to think that I'm advocating certain arrogance. Not so. It simply means holding your character and integrity in a place where courtesy and professionalism are not trumped by the pursuit of relationships, or getting people to like you. Being true to yourself is a job in itself, especially in difficult times.

In knowing yourself you can understand the attributes, skills, and sheer will that you bring to a place. You will also soon learn how much you don't know. It is this knowledge that leads you to learning and this is why change can be exciting, although stressful. Let the learning and growing override fear and stress. It is especially important to those of you just beginning your careers not to attach an air of entitlement or brash behavior to your action and name. Seasoned people around and above you will see right through this and you will bore them at best and amuse or turn them off at worst.

Acknowledge that you don't know it all, if even and only to yourself. Listen well and actively. Hear the tone and inflection and the reason for pause. Listen and speak the language and industry jargon of those above and around you. Respect the boundaries and rank of others while you learn and earn a place for yourself. Learn from history by taking a lesson from the experienced people who came before you. After all is said and done, there are probably 100 situations in business and they keep repeating. Everything old becomes new again, even in this time of geopolitical turmoil, new technology, downsizing, and Wall Street jitters. Other people have walked where you now walk. Learn from their experience, innovate to new heights, and thrive through change.

Respect the boundaries and rank of others while you learn and earn a place for yourself.

Being a consistent person and performer makes you a real haven for your manager's need for normalcy in tough times. Even some seasoned professionals with impressive track records act as if they are above the professional boundaries set in an office setting. I've often thought I'd take someone a little less excellent with strong growth potential if it meant less disruption for the team. I can remember managing a few people who were very good sellers but were also very temperamental. I could always count on one man in particular to disagree in an angry fashion in front of peers, yelling down a hallway, slamming doors and the like. He wanted to make his own calls on pricing and inventory without regard for the whole picture of supply and demand and he was resistant to any change in policy. Weaker members of the team would rally under his umbrella. He had the skills of a leader, but his energy was negative and rebellious. It took a lot of coaxing and coaching to get this employee to appreciate differing logic and comprehend the opportunities in new ways of doing things. In the end he became a positive leader, but the work and derailment were excruciating. Management challenges are a drain on energy and atmosphere that sometimes cost more than the extra market share from that type person. No one person is bigger than the total objective of the unit, division, or company overall.

Be enthusiastic and energetic in your knowledge seeking. Ask pertinent questions rather than opening your mouth just to be noticed. Read trades, network at industry functions, and brainstorm ideas with others. Be a sponge. Be unique. Be involved. Stretch yourself to learn about your industry, your customer needs, and the company's objectives. Be a standout among the crowd by actually thinking about what you do and why you're doing it. This sounds simple, but it is sorely lacking in many individuals. The answers to your analysis will lead you to new ideas. Be creative rather than rote. Think about what you're doing and what your customers, both internal and external, need and want. What will make their lives better? What will help them get a good night's sleep? You create value and a sense of fulfillment for yourself by being solution oriented and being known for getting things done. When customers, vendors, and company leaders identify you as a doer, your value will rise and you will feel real enjoyment in the accomplishment.

> *Be a standout among the crowd by actually thinking about what you do and why you're doing it. When customers, vendors, and company leaders identify you as a doer, your value will rise and you will feel real enjoyment in the accomplishment.*

One great way to keep in tune with your growth and value is to take time for a daily review. Perhaps you could make it part of your commute: Take stock of all you did that day. What went really well and what could have gone better? How much work were you able to handle well? Where did you spend too much time (i.e., pain vs. gain)? How did important exchanges with your manager, customer, or colleague go? What changes can you make tomorrow that will enhance your work and your pleasure? What are you learning about the work and yourself, the company, and its leaders? How is your workplace changing and how well are you able to accept the changes and become part of the leadership of that change? What constructive actions are you taking to keep values strong even through wild swings in objectives and temperament?

In the beginning of any new job your attributes are the skills, contacts, product knowledge, and resourcefulness that you bring. Lead with your strengths and work to learn which competencies matter the most in this environment. Work to improve the weaker sets to enhance your value and enjoyment. Don't be afraid to admit when you need clarity on a project. If you feel intimidated to ask your manager for help, than ask a member of your team whom you respect and are comfortable with. It is better to be sure than to be embarrassed.

> *It is better to be sure than to be embarrassed.*

Staying current with industry trends, language, computer software, new management philosophies, and the like is an important factor in keeping your value high. Take advantage of training offered by the company and also take the initiative on your own time for more learning to stay current. Enroll in courses at your local colleges and read business books and trade magazines so you can ride each tide of change, or even predict it before it happens.

Volunteer for new initiatives, even if it means a few more hours of work. Your interest will demonstrate a solid work ethic, dependability, adaptability, and willingness. Chances are you will be on a committee of valued thinkers and you can learn as much from them about the company and industry as you will about the new project. Be someone who can be depended on to embrace change and new policies or enterprise.

By understanding what motivates you, your core personal values, and the value you bring to an organization, you will be better informed to make smart decisions as you navigate your way. This is true in times that are stable and in times that require real change and adaptability. You will be less likely to let someone else's opinion of you become the sole or most important measure of your worth. By knowing these important values, you will more easily spot the people that you can freely respect, grow with, and be influenced by. Your own confidence and self-knowledge will help you decide whose opinion matters and this will guide you on your learning path from others.

Times, climate, leadership, and objectives change. You need to adapt to these changes to thrive, but you don't have to change the essence of who you are to succeed. Value yourself, stay in tune with the current climate and context, and take the high road when it comes to behavior you don't want to be part of. Value yourself, speak up when you need to, continue to deliver stellar work, and you will be more valuable to the company than you ever thought. Remember that you *are* very valuable. You have the power to make kings.

QUESTIONS

- What are your core values?

- What are the identified company values?

- How in sync are your values and those of the company?

- How well do you adapt to and manage change?

- How do you set boundaries about the way you'd like to be treated?

- How can you become a valuable standout in difficult times?

- How much do you trust your management to see through personality and value changes among the employee base during tough times?

■ Do you see that you might be more admired for staying true to yourself and applying yourself even more ardently to your work?

■ Does becoming more aware of your daily work help you better understand your progress?

■ Does daily awareness also help you improve and enjoy your work more?

■ Do your internal and external customers identify you as a solution-oriented person?

■ Do you keep yourself fresh through training, classes, trades, networking, and so on?

■ Do you value your opinion of yourself and choose whose measure you care about?

12 How Can You Affect the Company's Margin?

Incorporating the attributes of a profit contributor into your awareness and daily activity will enhance your value to the organization. Dollars saved can strengthen the research and development of new products, create new jobs, and be invested in capital improvements that will enhance the company's competitive standing, your job security, and the economy.

You can start by understanding the goal in the big-picture sense and then relating it to your own microview of your daily responsibilities. By finding ways of tying the macro (big picture) and micro (your desk) objectives together you will be delivering work that meets company goals in the fullest possible sense. By creating personal goals and measures and through awareness of your own processes, you will become a more conscious and efficient worker, and thus more valuable to the company. You could develop new standards for the entire organization by creating processes that measurably strengthen the road toward successful goal execution. This will bode well for you in many ways: for your heightened value as a visionary, thinker, and leader in the organization and for your own sense of fulfillment and entrepreneurship. All of the following suggestions could end up as real contributions and great additions to your champion and annual review files.

■ *Ask your manager to review as much of the business plan as he or she is comfortable exposing with you and your colleagues.*

Information is valuable. You'll have a better, bigger understanding of the objectives and the pressures on your manager that might come rolling your way. You'll gain insight that can lead to discovering and contributing measurable ideas that can result in gains for the company and for your future.

What are the revenue goals for your area, how do these tie into the division and company goals, and what are they based on? How does the company expect to reach its revenue and profit projections? Which areas of the company are posed for highest potential income increases? How can you become a part of those areas or projects?

■ *Which areas of the company will experience cost cuts and how will those cuts possibly impact revenue opportunity?*

For example, in television, when cuts are made in advertising and promotion, the ratings for a program are at risk and might subsequently yield lower prices for commercial airtime. Are there other areas for savings that you could recommend to keep revenue out of harm's way? What proof, in real numbers, can you present that will make your case strong? Is the idea provocative enough that your manager might want to add his or her suggestions, evaluation, and power to it?

> *Are there other areas for savings that you could recommend to keep revenue out of harm's way?*

■ *Keep a sharp eye on the cost side of your business plan.*

If you're not in charge of a business plan, make common-sense suggestions and propose activities that affect your area as part of your daily awareness and work. Your work, spending, and revenue are all part of the bigger business plan. (Budgets are written with a line devoted to each item, be it on the cost side or the revenue side. The bottom line of the cost analysis is subtracted from the revenue projection to reach the net revenue that leads to the company profit. The difference between the cost and the revenue is the profit margin.) The conundrum exists that if you spend less money on a certain line item than is allowed, your budget for that area could go down the following year. As a result, cost-side budgeting is sometimes purposely not squeezed to its greatest efficiency. Would it be reasonable for you to make suggestions that will help your area meet its part of the business plan overall, and less by line item, so that you can work the budget most effectively?

■ *Reduce excessive spending by testing vendor prices on a random basis and by inviting new competitors for your business.*

Minimize waste from paper to toner to salt in the cafeteria. Spend the company's money as if it were your own, unless, of course, you are a spendthrift.

■ *Hire well and work consciously to retain your key players.*

Each "head" counts for two now, so keep an eye out for people who are highly productive, creative, positive, and contribution driven. Keep this type of person happy because they're real commodities and replacement costs are very high. "Managing out" a bad hire requires time, costs sleep, and increases anxiety. People make profits and kings, so choose them wisely.

■ *Make your own area as efficient and organized as possible.*

One way is to create a process map for each of the tasks you handle. Write down the task and all the steps that it takes for you, and others involved, to deliver it. Look for redundancies in the steps and in the number of people who are doing the same thing, and move to streamline the work. It is a proven mathematical truth that the higher the number of people that touch a job, the higher the number of errors. Errors cost time and money and could cost customer confidence and future business as well. Streamlining the process will measurably tighten the results and

> *Streamlining the process will measurably tighten the results and could free overstressed people from multitasking where they don't need to.*

could free overstressed people from multitasking where they don't need to.

■ *Look for efficiency in the number of steps and the organization of your own personal area to reach steps and necessary information quickly.*

Physically move needed items to cut down on the time it takes to move from one step or task to another. Organize your computer and your desk so that the information you need for various tasks, or for general information, is easily accessible. This process will heighten your productivity, give you time to work on new and exciting projects and possibly shorten your day so that you can work on having a life. If you develop a process that can be duplicated across the office, take it to your manager for broader application. Once you become adept at managing your process and cutting redundancy you'll find that this skill permeates your whole life.

> *This process will heighten your productivity, give you time to work on new and exciting projects and possibly shorten your day so that you can work on having a life.*

Once I was at the cheese counter at Zabar's, a gourmet food store in New York City. I asked for a certain cheese. The salesperson had to walk from one end of the area all the way to the other to get to the cheese slicer, and then all the way back to the other end to wrap the cheese. It took everything in me not to shriek: Buy another slicer for this end of the counter or move the one you have to the middle! Cutting waste is better for the stressed employee; it saves money, time, customers and angst.

■ *Know the 80/20s of your business.*

This means that 80 percent of your business is likely to come from 20 percent of your customers. It takes as much time and energy to slay an elephant as it does to catch a kitten. You might as well use your time on the big ideas and deals if you can. Do give ample time and service to good customers and keep an eye out for breakout companies in the 20 percent rank that you can help to grow into the 80 percent group. Your suggestions and initiatives could give you and your company an inordinate market share once the company breaks out. Keep track of the growth on each piece of business so that you can merchandise it to your manager.

■ *Ask your customers for a road map to success.*

How do they like to conduct business? What worries them most? Which aspects of their jobs do they love and dislike most? Which competitors do they respect most and why? Hook in to their realities and become your customer's go-to person. Building a reputation as a person who gets things done is a key to higher sales, competitive information, and relationships that will transcend the workplace as you move up through the company or within your industry.

■ *Look out for redundancy or work no longer needed in the greater unit.*

Perhaps you are receiving several related reports that can be streamlined into one. Maybe you are writing or receiving reports because "they've always been done" and are past their usefulness. See which work is needed and which work is a duplicate or wasted effort. Make recommendations to your manager, including time and cost savings if you can. Let your observances and ensuing ideas make "cents" to the company.

■ *Don't be afraid to admit a mistake or nip one in the bud.*

It's a lot less embarrassing or devastating to be part of a thousand-dollar error before it becomes a million-dollar one.

Do it right the first time. No-half jobs are allowed in this house.

In the meantime two mantras that are worth storing in your brain are, from business, "Do it right the first time," and from my parents, "No-half jobs are allowed in this house." Mistakes or system glitches that cost time also cost you the opportunity to work on other items; they could also damage customer relationships and your credibility.

■ *Use your expense account wisely.*

I always preferred a face-to-face meeting, such as lunch or dinner or some other event, to sending a gift. I never sent or condoned "thank-you flowers" for an order because I believed that if the goal of a win for both parties was met, then the order was an asset to the buyer in and of itself. I discouraged flowers or food gifts or other expense items as a thank you because I wanted the salespeople to have face time with their customers to build relationships. I believed gifts could actually cheapen the dignity of the salesperson and the work. Obviously there are always exceptions to any rules; just use your best judgment and have dignity about it.

■ *Celebrating success is a welcomed tool for morale and consistent performance.*

Whether lunch in or an off-site outing, the message is clear: Thank you, you count, let's keep winning. Companies have various rules regarding the use of expense accounts for internal use, so be sure to check yours before incurring costs. Sometimes your own splurge on some pizzas and beers will yield a healthy return on investment.

How can you affect the company profit from any job position and what's in it for you? Learn what is needed and do what you can to fill the need from your spot. As a leader or an up-and-coming one, strive to be observant and set good examples. Make it your goal to know your business and grow your efficiency and awareness and soon it will just become part of the valuable employee that you are known to be. Nothing feels better than to be on top of your game with people, profit, product, and services all humming along at once.

Celebrating success is a welcomed tool for morale and consistent performance.

QUESTIONS

■ Do you regularly think beyond the requested work to fully understand the bigger picture?

■ Is your work world efficient? Are there improvements that you can suggest to either cut redundancy or improve process?

■ Are you a part of a unit that is integral to revenue building for the company? Can you influence this goal by other means if you are not in that area? How?

■ Do your customers know that you are a person who understands their pressure and gets things done in a win–win way?

■ Do you keep spending at current levels because you don't want to suffer cuts next year? Is it feasible to talk to your manager of finance about reaching the bottom line of the budget in the whole-picture sense versus line by line?

■ What work is redundant in your area? What suggestions can you make that will result in streamlining, cost savings, and time savings?

■ Do you celebrate success enough?

13 BECOME YOUR MANAGER'S GO-TO PERSON

The clearest way to become a valuable member of a team is to have measurable results and to deliver what your manager needs in the format requested, covering every item succinctly, on time and without problems, on a consistent basis. Consistency is key to trust building and comfort level between you and your manager. I always found great comfort in knowing my go-to people would never let me down. They would push new ideas, suggest better processes, and fill in my blind spots. I would learn from them and they would learn from and enjoy the experience. I loved being my boss's go-to person. I was able to work on projects outside of my normal scope and I grew as a result. This is an incredible win–win result. Earn your spot as a go-to person; it will make you stronger as a leader, worker, and whole, thinking person.

A good way to deliver complete and breakthrough work is to anticipate the specific tasks involved in the creation of the work and to prepare in advance for each item. Understanding why a goal is the goal is the first step; this helps to stretch your thinking on a subject. Ponder and ask how this action affects the division's overall goals. How will this movement affect your competition, your customers, and your compensation? How will the execution of this goal affect

> *Ill-prepared work will cost you time and embarrassment, frustrate your boss, and reflect badly on you.*

the company's overall growth and profit margin? Ask for clarity when you need it rather than taking a chance and delivering work that is off the mark. Ill-prepared work will cost you time and embarrassment, frustrate your boss, and reflect badly on you.

Think backwards and work forward. Acknowledge the goal in full by thinking of all the components and writing down the needed parts to fulfill it. Set an action timeline, one section at a time, with due dates, leading you to delivery of the final goal. In this way, your work is focused and you have an early sense of the time it will take for you to complete each task. You will also realize the resources you have available or will need for each step. You can be working on step one while gathering information needed for step three. Your work will be complete and on time, and might offer some breakthrough suggestions for the broader good.

If you have ideas that you believe will enhance the final product but are outside the request, ask your manager how you should proceed. It might be necessary to complete the work as requested and deliver a separate document at the same time, or you might be invited to discuss your idea verbally to see how it fits or improves the work. It is valuable and exhilarating to feel the freedom to make suggestions, but you must learn the ways to do this in the environment and timeline that the manager is directing. Do not just go ahead and add your spin to the report because more is not always better to a busy person.

> *Missing a deadline without advance notice to the manager is a major irritant that could brand you as a problem. Nothing is more deadly than losing a deal or making a critical call without informing and gaining input from your manager.*

Missing a deadline without advance notice to the manager is a major irritant that could brand you as a problem. If you are having trouble juggling priorities, then ask for a discussion to go through your projects to prioritize. You might gain insight into what is really most pressing and you might also find that you could buy yourself valuable time on a deadline. Remember that you are not the only one who is overloaded. For every report you are asked to write, your manager must compile and analyze reports from the entire team and create an overview report for his or her own manager. Think beyond your own spot.

Nothing is more deadly than losing a deal or making a critical call without informing and gaining input from your manager. We used to say, "Don't go down alone." Be sure your work is thorough and that you've done all you can up to the block point; then bring it to the business leader with suggestions to solve the problem if you can. Don't go down alone if you expect to be backed in a disappointing situation.

I remember one deal from long ago. A fellow received a lower than expected share on a piece of business because he had too many live deals on his desk, some for larger markets with bigger budgets. He felt so awful about it, he was reticent to call it in. He sat on the deal for three days. I saw where we could have packaged more aggressively or priced more competitively if he'd brought the deal to me for further negotiation. That was one problem. The other was that by waiting to report the order, there was no way that we could go back to the buyer for reconsideration. The time lapse was enough that the orders to the other stations in the market were placed and any real hope for a turnaround went with them. The budgets he did well on were good for the company overall, but this was a relatively large budget for my market and this specific television station. The negligence and apprehension was expensive, unnecessary, and unfortunate. The good news is that the story was not repeated.

Acknowledge your partnership and respect for the leadership in your company while you show your customers that they are important to your organization.

Don't be a hero or a territorial separatist. Include your manager on customer calls or in meetings with equally high-level counterparts. Acknowledge your partnership and respect for the leadership in your company while you show your customers that they are important to your organization. Bringing your manager along on a sales call or to an important meeting will also give you an opportunity to showcase your work.

If you are in a situation where you need or want to give feedback to your manager, give it professionally. Ask for a meeting and go to it ready to discuss the problem and how it affects the work and the team. Don't whine, complain, or speak in negative or inflammatory language. Lead with a positive attitude and always try to bring a solution to the problem so that it isn't a problem for long. This initiative will set you apart as it displays your investment in quality work and the working environment.

Language is very important. Take great care to present yourself in the way in which you want to be portrayed. Take as much charge as you can of the perceptions that will form your reputation and inform your career growth. If you aspire to a level beyond the one you are in, yet you speak in a way that riles people or is alarmist, you will hurt your long-term chances. If you are a woman and you use words like "honey" and "sweetie" (at least in New York) you could undermine your own authority. If you use foul language or scream and shout, it will reflect on your seeming lack of vocabulary, polish and personal control. Leadership, in great part, depends on your ability to articulate your vision in a motivating fashion. Some words do not belong in business; monitor your mouth so that you speak the way you want to be recognized.

> *Leadership, in great part, depends on your ability to articulate your vision in a motivating fashion. Some words do not belong in business; monitor your mouth so that you speak the way you want to be recognized.*

A clear path to success is to ensure your own area is efficient, organized, smart, and revenue generating, cost reducing, or both. Becoming known for these competencies will help you gain access to fun and important projects, increase your chances of securing a great champion, and keep your career growing.

All of these steps will enhance your value and gain your manager's trust. You will be the person he or she can count on in a pinch, or brainstorm with to move something that is acceptable to something that is outstanding. The best part is that you will learn so much! You will learn about big-picture thinking, problem solving, articulating a vision, teamwork, the honor of great work, and fantastic results will rule. You will learn what you are made of, and that is bankable stuff.

QUESTIONS

- Is your work timely and complete on a consistent basis?

- Are you comfortable asking for clarity on a project?

- Are you invested in your work enough to make enhancement suggestions?

- Do you include your manager in customer calls, difficult negotiations, or important meetings?

- Are you solution oriented?

- Are you a consistent performer? Are you results oriented with an eye on the process it takes to get there?

- What steps can you take to become someone your manager can rely on in a pinch?

14 Getting a Handle on Obsession and Defensive Action

We worry about many issues during our working life. We concern ourselves with the way we are perceived and the way we are treated. We care what our boss will think about our work and obsess over a thoughtless remark thrown our way that the speaker wouldn't even remember, while pondering politics, positioning, and the exact right words to say. We are disquieted about attribution, appreciation, and being a player in the place and invest ourselves in current projects as we think about our future. We worry about far too much; the negative energy wipes out creativity and productivity and steals our very center away from us. We want dignity and integrity to be lead qualities of our workplace in order to achieve heightened productivity and learning, and we obsess when those values are insulted or at risk.

We worry about far too much; the negative energy wipes out creativity and productivity and steals our very center away from us.

There is everything right about realizing what matters to you and protecting those identified values as much as possible. There is a harmful aspect if you overthink a subject, however. By gaining a handle on your own thinking you can get through the obstacles more easily. It is important to have a clear vision of the situation so that you can evaluate and take action or let it go. Following are a few sample situations and recommendations for quieting your mind.

■ *My boss is always throwing out cynical or sarcastic remarks and my feelings get hurt.*

Are you being singled out or is this just the way this person works and speaks? If this is his or her general temperament, see how your colleagues feel about the situation and ask them what they do to avoid personalizing it. If you think you are being treated differently than the others you have at least three choices.

- You can go directly to the person and ask if you've done anything to incur this wrath and communicate the way that you'd like to be treated.
- You can go to human resources and enter a complaint.
- You can realize that this person is just "that way" and you don't really care what he or she thinks about you beyond your performance appraisal.

In any case, you might come to the realization that this action is not at all about you. The sarcasm could be an attempt at humor or it could be a manifestation of a belief that keeping a distance between levels and cold intimidation is a great management tool. When you realize that this is about the other person, you can relax and understand that you are probably not going to see a huge personality shift any time soon. As long as your work and your future are not compromised, do your best to let it go. If, however, the remarks are relentless and pointed, do take some action. You'll feel better about yourself and this person might grow in the bargain.

■ *I tend to read into remarks and make things worse than they are.*

Here's an example. Someone I know tried to reach his manager at headquarters to let him know he had to leave "early." Early, in this case, was 6:30 in the evening. He couldn't reach his boss, but left word via e-mail and through his administrative assistant that he was leaving, but reachable by cell phone. The next morning he opened his e-mail and received a message from his manager, that read, "I'd appreciate knowing when you have to leave early." My friend was aghast and angry, probably the result of feeling needlessly guilty. "How dare he question me when I tried to reach him two ways? I work like a dog for this guy and he just doesn't get it! How dare he tell me I can't go to my son's soccer game?"

Think about this: The manager was under intense pressure at the time and he needed the comfort of knowing his key players were reachable. Perhaps he didn't get the message, or the message reached him at exactly the wrong time. Nowhere did the manager say this person wasn't appreciated; on the contrary: knowing he could be reached was a comfort to him. Any mention of the child's soccer game was a complete fabrication on the recipient's part.

Sometimes you might set a mental videotape in motion and lose all the qualities and control of the movie director. The thing just flies off in your mind and you manage to wind yourself into one big, obsessive knot. A better idea might be to take a deep breath and think about the messenger's mental place when the upsetting statement was made. Another recommendation is to stop the tape. Take a walk around the block and consider the situation from all angles. You might even realize that you matter more than you thought to your management.

■ *I made a fool of myself in that meeting. I wasn't prepared, didn't know my material, and tried to fake my way through it. They saw right through me!*

Was it really as bad as all that or are you being very hard on yourself? Ask a trusted colleague for perceptions of how you presented yourself. You might learn that you appeared better than you thought. In the heat of a moment you might not realize that you have more specific and direct product knowledge than the people you report to and when this is the case, the gaffe is not so apparent. You can always follow through with a memo to restate your points and add pertinent support data, or even add an appropriate and fresh viewpoint based on the discussion in the meeting.

Nothing works for your confidence better than knowing the product information cold and simply admitting when you don't know something. Faking your way through anything is a pitfall that will find you awash in embarrassment and lost credibility. Don't do it. Be the best at what you do because you are thorough. If you make it a priority to be as prepared as possible and a meeting still goes badly, at least your work won't be doubted and your credibility will not be questioned. If you don't know something, admit it, take copious notes, and pledge to answer the question immediately after the meeting, then be sure to deliver.

■ *I wasn't even considered for that promotion. I am not on the radar screen. I feel invisible and not important to the organization.*

First, make a checklist of actions that could ensure that you won't feel this way again: Had you made your career goals clear to your management and to human resources? Has your management been showcasing your work to upper management? Was the promotion open to interviews or was it filled slam-dunk? Does it make sense beyond cronyism that the job went to someone else? Is this the first time this has happened?

If you lose a bid for a new post, have a talk with your manager to gain a better understanding of the result. Be calm and clear about your goals and ask if you are understood and if your plans sound achievable. If appropriate to your company culture, ask for a meeting with your HR person to discuss your disappointment and your goals. You might learn why that other person was hired over you or you might learn why you weren't considered, if that was the case. Sometimes, just stating your intentions is enough to get you on the screen. Ask questions even if you are afraid of the answer. You can't fix something if you don't know what the problem is.

Sometimes, just stating your intentions is enough to get you on the screen.

You might take this as an opportunity to assess different ways that can raise your stature and your perceived value. What crucial initiative is happening in the company right now that you can become a part of? In what ways can you contribute to immediate forward action that will result in a gain for the company and move you onto the radar? You might learn that there is a perceived or real style differential that hampers the comfort zone between the hiring manager and you. It's fine to be angry and disappointed, but it is not fine to pout or obsess without taking action.

■ *An important customer call occurred and I was not invited, even though I've been working on the deal for months. I have been left out of customer entertainment events even though my position and current work dictates my inclusion. The same person has been involved in these exclusions and I am beginning to get a knot in my stomach every time I see him. I am beginning to feel isolated and frozen out.*

If you are left out of important face time, to which you have a legitimate right with customers—internal or external—you have a right to take action. Action is healthier than an ulcer. You have a few choices to make. First, go directly to the person who is undermining you and ask why this is happening. Be as calm as you can and even write a private note card with important points so that you don't miss one in case nerves or anger take over. Bring specific examples of the slights and the exact reasons why you should have been included. Tell this person why your inclusion is essential to the objective's success and what your expectations are. See if you can create a new set of guidelines for future action.

If this person is not responsive, or gives you lip service while continuing to exclude you, go to the next level of management. Explain the situation, detail the ensuing detriment to the company objectives and to your morale, and ask for help in changing the situation. At the least, you will expose the person and find out how next-tier management reacts to the issues of exclusion, politics, lack of teamwork, and your unhappiness with this situation.

If you are still not satisfied with the results, go to human resources. Don't be afraid. You are going on record as a contributing and concerned member of the company who sees a misdemeanor that is defiant of company charter, business, and human relations. You are exposing the person's politics and your own philosophies and you want answers and a change in action. These are honorable questions as long as you are sure that you are in the right and are not exaggerating the issue.

If isolation and undermining occurs, realize that you are a perceived threat to the one who is undercutting you. It's a backhanded, hurtful compliment to be sure, even if it feels terrible. You are working on something that has merit and they might want to make it their own. Do your best to nip this in the bud.

The difficult and real risk here is that you could be driven to change into someone who is not desirable or in concert with your values. This would include becoming exclusive by hoarding information until a deal is closed, not trusting your coworkers, breaking off from the team, and creating your own isolation as a way of coping. This sort of situation could lead you to feeling and acting covetous, greedy, and suspicious. This is not fun, nor is it healthy. Don't become like the person who knotted your stomach in the first place. Continue to work and share and be the leader you are while you continue to expose action that is unbecoming. Remember that great work and excellent results are the greatest revenge in the long run; keep your eye on your long-term propositions to get you through the near-term angst.

If this sort of atmosphere permeates your work environment, you have some choices to make. You will have to find a way to work within these rules or identify a place you want to go to and create a plan to get there before you are hurt. How long will the villain be in place? Does this person have upper management's backing? Were your issues met with concern and action or largely ignored? If ignored, did you at least gain an understanding about why this type of action is acceptable? Can you live with it?

■ *I have new management due to internal movement (or a company takeover). After a few months I can see that I am not one of the new manager's "people." I'm feeling threatened, insecure, and as if my ideas and suggestions are not heard or valued. Rather than putting my energy into new or current work, I find my mind drifting uncontrollably, obsessing about the situation and worrying for my future.*

Do your best to objectively assess the situation at hand. Do you have specific examples of not being heard or being left out? Are you being treated differently than the group you perceive to be on the inside? Is the new boss inundated with new responsibilities? Are you in an area that is working well and not in need of immediate attention? Are your management peers receiving help in the form of capital improvements or resources that you're not getting, and does this make you feel less important or your area less imperative? Are you in good stead in the company? Have you felt appreciated and has this been manifested in good reviews and raises? Are you willing to leave if your insecurities and instincts are not resolved? How easy will it be to get another fulfilling job? What other companies do you admire? Do you have contacts there? Start to prepare a mental Plan B so that you have some action steps ready in case the floor falls from under your feet.

After you have paid attention to the listed questions, ask for a meeting with the new manager. Let he or she know that you appreciate the recent ramp-up pressure and discuss positively any new policies that you are truly keen on. Be calm and prepared: Have your note card with your key points and agenda ready to aid you. Let the manager know that you are coming from a place of great caring, that you enjoy your work and the company and want to remain a contributing member. Then you can go into your request for a confidence affirmation. Let the leader know the slights you have felt personally, or to your department, with specific examples of the incidents. Ask for the manager's priority list so that you can gain a better understanding of why your requests have not been filled.

> By putting yourself on the line, you have a lot to gain: the respect of your manager, insights into departmental priorities and pressures, and an understanding of where you really fit and how you are viewed.

Check your tone and insecurity at the door; you've already put yourself through the wringer and have taken a courageous step by asking for this meeting. You have nothing to lose because you understand your value to the company and to your industry. By putting yourself on the line, you have a lot to gain: the respect of your manager, insights into departmental priorities and pressures, and an understanding of where you really fit and how you are viewed. You will also contribute to making this person a better manager because he or she might not have had any idea that you felt slighted in the midst of working so hard on his or her own new job.

If you learn that you are not part of the new team, you will feel a blow even if you knew it in the pit of your stomach the whole time. Ask if and how this might be corrected and take the time to decide if you are willing to make the desired changes. Perhaps the problem is one of perception and you can change it rather simply. If any salvation seems moot, discuss the manager's intent, ask for time, start thinking about severance, and start on your Plan B.

The morals of these examples are few but important. Communication is key, including the way you talk to yourself. Take the time to consider a troubling situation from all angles so that you will be more prepared to take action or be able to live with it more easily. Speak up for yourself in a way that is logical, unemotional, and clear. Perception is reality; you need to understand how others see you so that you can create a view that you deserve and agree with.

If you expect specific behavior from certain people, don't be surprised when it happens and take it in stride as much as possible. Realize that politics and change are constant and that excellent work is your only real security. No matter what is happening on the inside, take care of your customers or vendors on the outside. Be the solution-oriented professional with great contacts because your marketplace could help you to secure your next position. This happened to me and I will never forget the customers who spoke for me even before I did or asked them to. Their generosity carried me through a difficult time and made the experience actually sweet.

Realize that politics and change are constant and that excellent work is your only real security.

It is not easy to confront a bad situation. For me, the worst was feeling "frozen out," or purposely isolated. There was a short period of time when I was not invited to a few important company functions when I worked at vice president level running the sales area of an important new company initiative. The exposure to key clients would have well served our company in this new enterprise. I went directly to the person who handled the occasions and the trips and he put it off by saying that I was not a direct report of his and therefore my invitation was not his responsibility. Collaboration was not the priority that politics and dominion were to this person. Taking this to the next level meant I had to bother my president, who had much more important things to deal with than a petty invitation list. However, it wasn't petty to me and it wasn't just a matter of the invitation. Salespeople who indirectly reported to me were included and I was shunned. I felt this was a conscious slight (especially after I confronted the person) enveloped in a territorial maneuver that put me in a bad place mentally, emotionally, and politically. Why was I put in this ridiculous place? I was incredulous, I was hurt, and I was really angry. My president invited me to a most important function, but this seemed beside the point because, to my knowledge, the root cause of my distress, being purposely left out, was not addressed head-on. Satisfaction at being included was only half-full because the action of exclusion, in and of itself, was not brought out into the open and solved. I imagine an "alliance dance," a bit of a nod between the president and the excluder that said, "Hey, knock it off", but it was too little too late and this spoke volumes to me.

When I finally went to my management to let them know I wanted to leave, I cited this as one of the many silent degradations I could no longer live with. The human resource person I met with listened with a raised eyebrow and I knew she understood and agreed. Sometimes hindsight might be 20/20, but it is not a cure-all. Stopping negative behavior over territorialism or another hidden agenda while it is happening will go a long way to retain valuable employees.

> *Stopping negative behavior over territorialism or another hidden agenda while it is happening will go a long way to retain valuable employees.*

If you find yourself in a place that you have tried to improve and nothing is working, speak kindly to yourself as you make your decisions. Ask yourself what you're worth and what this is doing to your morale and your own view of yourself. Don't doubt yourself if you have a track record and if you know that you are valuable. Realize that the dilemma isn't about your value to the company; instead, you might be an unaware threat to someone who has his or her own agenda, as well as backing and power within the company. Write lists, meditate, and practice the acting lesson to come up with a person or place in the universe that has the competencies that you have always had but just forgot. Talk to your personal "board of directors," those people you trust and count on when you are faced with difficult life decisions. Stand up for yourself and, if necessary, let it be their loss, not yours. You are valuable and you deserve to be treated with all of the respect you have earned. Go get a job with good people who deserve you.

> *Stand up for yourself and let it be their loss, not yours. You are valuable and you deserve to be treated with all of the respect you have earned. Go get a job with good people who deserve you.*

QUESTIONS

- What do you obsess over? Do you spot a consistent theme?

- What is the cause of your insecurity? What is at your core that manifests itself in obsession and defense?

- Do you take responsibility for your actions and reactions or do you put it on other people?

- What can you do, in terms of priority or time management, to be sure that you are always completely prepared before a meeting?

- How do you feel about confrontational action? What sort of preparation can help steel your courage?

- Would you rather be "safe" and unhappy or free and happy?

- What are you doing to ensure that you have the backing in the marketplace and in your bank account to take a risk that might cost you your job?

- How much difficulty can you live with before you start to change from the person you love into someone you don't even recognize? What is worth this?

- Do you realize that your managers are not omniscient and that if you have a track record for good judgment, solid results, and unquestionable ethics, you are more likely to be heard?

- Have you done everything possible to make a difficult situation more palatable?

- Does empathy with a manager's situation and stress level help you to see the issue more clearly, perhaps to your advantage?

15 WHEN IS IT OKAY TO BREAK RANK?

Time magazine celebrated the courage and integrity of the whistle-blower by naming three important movers of 2002 the "Persons of the Year": Cynthia Cooper of Worldcom, Colleen Rowley of the FBI, and Sherron Watkins of Enron. Many have gone before these women and many will follow.

Fitzgerald, Wigand, Nader, and Silkwood are names of famous whistle-blowers that could not keep quiet in the face of what they believed to be great wrongdoing. The issues at hand were varied and important, including government waste in the form of a $7,000 coffee maker, cigarette manufacturers denying addictive qualities, a car that could harm millions, and health hazards in a nuclear power plant.

These people could not pretend that all was well. They went above and beyond the place of the worker, to the place of exemplary citizenship, in conscious awareness of the risks and rewards related to their personal core values. Each of these people and countless, uncelebrated others like them understood the risks involved. They surely had to sublimate ego and fear to carry out their missions, as job loss, industry blackballing, and unwanted notoriety were just some of the possible scenarios they faced.

These examples are extreme, but you might find yourself in a position where you see that something is amiss and you will deliberate taking action. Listen to yourself and decide how much the subject matters to you on a core level and to the company on a broader one. Examine your standing with your manager. Are you trusted as a contributory member of the team? Have you shown good judgment on a consistent basis through other tough calls? Are you known to make suggestions regularly that have proven substantial, or are you someone who causes alarm by complaining without suggestions for

> The standing you hold, and the trust covenant you and your management forge, will make a major difference in the way your suggestions are heard and acted on.

improvement? The standing you hold, and the trust covenant you and your management forge, will make a major difference in the way your suggestions are heard and acted on.

Sometimes bringing an important issue to your manager's attention will not yield the response you hope for. Perhaps the manager doesn't want to get his or her hands dirty, or this leader does not want to get involved in something that could open up a can of political worms with senior management. What should you do? Let your stomach, or other bodily stress point, be your guide. Your instincts will tell you when you cannot sit on the truth.

I was career-raised in the post-Vietnam era when "chain of command" and other military rules abounded. We were told to follow the chain and not to usurp the leadership, and most of the time things were taken care of pretty well. I can think of a few situations in which I took issues to my management or even higher, and they usually centered on personnel issues, such as sexual harassment, bullying, making fun of someone on my team, and so on. I couldn't sit still for demeaning action and I don't believe I hurt myself by standing up to it. On the other hand, I would have hurt myself more by denying the truth and failing to take action because that would be living out of concert with my values.

My choice, most of the time, was to talk it out with the people involved. I'd go to my manager one-on-one and try to explain the ramifications of a certain action to the person involved and to the team at large.

A somewhat amusing story is another example of breaking rank. It was the time of the Gulf War in 1991 and I was working for FOX. I was number two in the sales department and Rupert Murdoch's Australians surrounded us as consultants, working in concert with our new-to-television GM. They brought many innovative ideas and programs, but early on they might not have always understood some of our cultural nuances and how cutthroat the competitive nature of local market television in the United States could be. Sometimes you have to risk short-term revenue in order to advance ideals such as serving your constituency of viewers and being the news leader in your market.

I met some friends at a local pub after work; the place was crowded and full of noise and activity. The television sets were tuned to ABC, CBS, and NBC and they each had preempted prime-time programming for news coverage of the war. The pictures showed Israelis in gas masks as the announcers spoke of the latest moves commanded by President George Bush. A friend was reading aloud from a book of Winston Churchill's speeches and people were talking war. The pitch was torqued up every few seconds; the place was full and frenzied. I asked the bartender to turn one of the sets to Channel 5 to view our coverage for a minute and was aghast to see that we were airing *The Simpsons*.

We were airing a prime-time cartoon while our competition brought the war into our viewers' living rooms! I could understand the thinking: *The Simpsons* brought in some of the highest prime-time ratings for then-nascent FOX, and was an important commercial revenue source for us. On the other hand, I feared no one was watching our station because they were watching the war. I needed to do something! I wasn't sure where my boss was and this was at a time before people were attached to cell phones, pagers, Blackberry, and so on. I took a deep breath and called the station and asked for the GM, who was in the newsroom monitoring the war on the competition, deliberating our next move with the news director consultant. She took my call and I basically and bluntly asked why we were running a cartoon when Israel was on fire. I reminded her that our constituency included many Jewish people who were possibly related to the very people in those gas masks. I cringed nervously and pulled my hair as I heard the unimaginable answer, *"Nothing new is really happening yet; it's just pictures of people in gas masks."* I mumbled this again to myself to see if I'd really heard it and dove into a fast and hard plea. I hastily explained that if anything "more" newsworthy did happen, no one would know to turn to us anyway. Since the viewership level watching *The Simpsons* would be quite a bit lower than normal, we'd have to "make good" the time anyway, meaning that keeping *The Simpsons* on the air was not going to prove to be profitable.

I made an urgent request to take the station to the CNN feed and thankfully they did so within seconds. I'm sure they were ready to go and I simply helped to push them over the edge, but seeing a cartoon on the air nearly pushed me over the edge! Even though I knew I did the right thing, I was very nervous about what I'd just done. I jumped over my boss and I didn't think he'd be too happy with me. However, on a deeper personal level, I needed to know that I worked for a television station that served the market. It was about revenue and profit, but our license was to serve. I'd learned early in my career that news was sacrosanct and I wanted to work for a place that served that honor. (Note: As of Q1 2002, Fox News Channel was the top-rated cable news service in the country. The local FOX station in New York has a very competitive news niche and has, for years, preempted regular programming for important breaking news.)

My boss called me into his office the next morning and asked me about my call to our GM as he nonchalantly shined his shoes and averted my eyes. I explained my reasons and the urgency I felt about our lack of coverage and the low risk to the revenue. I reiterated our contract with the viewer. He was a TV veteran and very aware of what a commitment to news meant. He let me speak and then just said, "OK." I didn't get into any trouble and our TV station served the market well.

I look back on this as a great experience. I went beyond rank for the greater good of the television station and the market and it worked out. I believe it worked because it was right, there was no malicious intent in the action, and my manager trusted my instincts and intentions. I was exhilarated. It's only now, more than a decade later, and through this writing that I see that I was worried about a reprimand and hadn't even thought about the appreciation for the action that didn't come. Isn't that quite something? What is the moral of this story as I see it today? Let your conviction and instinct be your guide. If you are a person in good standing in terms of judgment and ethics, people will be less likely to block your effort, even if they don't give you a big cheer along the way.

If you are a person in good standing in terms of judgment and ethics, people will be less likely to block your effort, even if they don't give you a big cheer along the way.

Not all breakout action has to be dramatic. If you are a person who treats the company as if it were your own, then you are in for some fun and possibly some raised eyebrows from those around you. Many times while viewing from home, I'd call the newsroom if I saw a misspelling on the horizontal news crawl. Why not help the company present itself in the best possible light? These little actions were private, because nobody had to know that I was the caller, and it gave me a fun sense of satisfaction.

I always loved programming and strategizing the marketing and sales of a prime-time schedule. I once suggested that a network sneak-peak an important prime-time fall show premiere in a hot time period reserved for a long-running, very popular program. My own manager thought the suggestion would never fly and that I was out of place to make it. Nonetheless, I asked his permission to submit the idea to the vice president of network programming and he gave it to me. The network ran the new program in the strong time period and it garnered the highest ratings for a prime-time premier in the network's history up to that date. My manager and our GM read the letter I'd written to the sales force, and they took me out for lunch to celebrate conviction. The network programmer never acknowledged my suggestion, and perhaps others had the idea, too. I would have enjoyed that attribution, and the lack of it made the experience a tad flat beyond my manager's generosity and my own personal satisfaction. In any case, it was a great exercise in making something better through a spark of an idea.

If you see something that you perceive to be wrong, or could be enhanced and you feel it in the pit of your stomach, do something about it. If you first go to your manager and he or she chooses not to do anything about it, ask if you can. If the answer is still negative and you are committed to the issue, let your manager know that though you respect his or her view you still feel very strongly about it and would like to take further action. A manager worth his or her salt will try to understand your view and either agree to take action or give you the blessing to do so.

> *You will inform yourself about your own values and you will learn much about the integrity of your company and its leaders.*

If your supervisor tries to stop you and you are not stoppable, go ahead and do the right thing anyway. You can do this in a way that will not incriminate your manager, but it will certainly inform the leaders of the company about your character. Best of all, you will inform yourself about your own values and you will learn much about the integrity of your company and its leaders. If you stay silent you take the chance of hurting your company, your objectives, your team, and yourself.

Remember, though, that there is risk involved that must be considered.

QUESTIONS

- How important is the subject of your discontent?

- What will the company gain from your action?

- What will you gain by taking action?

- How much are you willing to lose by taking this action?

- Does your manager trust your motivation and intent?

- How will your direct manager feel about you moving ahead with your report if he or she is against the action?

- Will you be reprimanded overtly or covertly for taking action?

- Would you be willing to lose your job or decide to look for work elsewhere over this issue?

- Can you live with yourself if you take no action?

16 INTERVIEW DISCOVERY

No matter your level, you are always in a building mode, developing a solid foundation or adding a growth pattern to your career in the form of the companies you work for and the people you learn from. It will be helpful in your assessment to know what you liked best about your last post, what new learning or environment would be exciting to you, and why you want this job in this company at this time. Writing a list of desired attributes in the company and competencies in its leadership will help you in your first phase of investigation.

> *No matter your level, you are always in a building mode, developing a solid foundation or adding a growth pattern to your career in the form of the companies you work for and the people you learn from.*

It is important that you take the organization's reputation into account when you are evaluating which company to join. Affiliation with top-ranking corporations might enhance your value throughout the industry. Excellent leadership, training, innovation, and degree of difficulty all transcend the fast checkpoints such as income. Companies that are most desired are those that develop and advance their high-potential people.

It shouldn't be difficult to identify the companies you'd be most interested in. Use your awareness of the competition as a first step. Ask your customers and people you've met at network associations for their take on specific companies and people. Look up past *Fortune* issues to read up on the Top 100 companies to work for. Run a computer search for the best companies in your industry. If you are a woman or minority, search with these specifics in mind as well.

After you have targeted companies, completed your research diligence, and secured an interview, your investigation can go further when you get to the office.

Get to the appointment 15 minutes early so you can sit in the lobby and observe. What does the office feel like? Are people happy, moving, and talking? Is there action and positive energy? Is it quiet, careful, and sterile? Does the place feel tense or energetic? Are people industrious or are they playing computer games? What do their faces look like? Are they scrunched in stress or relaxed and focused? Is the place too calm? Do people smile and say "hello" to each other as they pass in the hallways? Do people walk with some urgency or saunter down the hall? How are people dressed and does it fit the business? Is the environment clean and organized? Do you see loads of paper in a paperless world? Is the phone ringing? Does this feel like a place you could enjoy working in?

There are many ways to find your answers to questions about values, quality of life, work, stress, innovation, communication, and teamwork.

Find out if there is a mission statement for the division. What is it and how was it derived? Does the mission statement reflect the core values of the area, which will give you clues to the leadership and environmental disposition? Who were the parties involved in building the statement? Who are the key stakeholders in the division? How well does your manager work with these others? The answers to these questions will tell you a lot about this person as a team player and a consensus builder, and they will also give you a sense of his or her political savvy and involvement.

> *There are many ways to find your answers to questions about values, quality of life, work, stress, innovation, communication, and teamwork.*

Ask about the employee turnover in this area. If it is high, ask why: Are there morale problems or are people being promoted from this division?

Determine if the company has a succession management plan. Are competencies identified for each level? Are steps to promotion within the company clear? Is this a meritocracy (where great work transcends cronyism) and can that be proven? What are the possibilities for growth and track from the position you are interviewing for? What is the company's outlook and track record on diversity in hiring and promotions?

Information technology should be discussed during the interview. Which resources, in the form of reports and software, are available to you? What are the processes and reports that you will be working with? What is the state of the technology department? Is there adequate support staff for the area? Do multiple systems communicate with each other? Ease of data capture could be critical to your new role; if it is, find out if it's in good shape or what hurdles it might represent.

It is best to leave compensation to the final stages of the interview process. Use the time in your first sessions to learn about the company culture and the person to whom you will be reporting. Use the time to represent yourself in the truest possible light so that a match has the highest opportunity to portend well for your future within the company. Get the offer first and let the compensation outcome follow. You gain leverage in pay when the employer is sure you are the person they want to hire. You become the "get" and the hiring manager has probably talked you up to the next level of management. Once your name is mentioned internally, the negotiation takes on a new dimension to this person. You would have done some homework by that point and would have an idea of the compensation range for the open job so that you're not in the dark going in.

You gain leverage in pay when the employer is sure you are the person they want to hire. Once your name is mentioned internally, the negotiation takes on a new dimension to this person.

If you discuss money at the first meeting you are at risk of turning the hiring manager off. This might seem to be a gross generalization, but I often found people motivated first by money some of the most difficult people to manage. Stripped of other mental or emotional stimulation, everything comes down to dollars and cents, or the "what's in it for me" attitude. When money is the chief influence, the person is likely to measure accomplishment and fulfillment from his or her pay-check, rather than the contribution required in achieving it. Mine was a sales and marketing career, and salespeople who were dollar dominated, especially those on commission, some-times brought in deals that benefited their pocket more than the company. This created a real management challenge because customer relations, budgets, and inventory could be compromised, and unwarranted diligence over these deals was time wasted. Energy better placed elsewhere was spent on rejecting or reworking deals, teaching why, soothing custom-ers, and other untimely work.

Most strong leaders want to hire people with a will to learn and win, who are able to manage change, and who are inven-tive and strive for promotion and growth. These competencies are val-ued by great organizations and the best candidates understand that money, stock options, and other benefits are a very important part of the deal, but not the whole deal. The understanding is that as your value to an organization and an industry grows, so will your W2 and 401(k).

The understanding is that as your value to an organization and an industry grows, so will your W2 and 401(k).

When the compensation conversation occurs, be prepared and alert. If you are applying for a straight salary job, know the range for your level before you go into the negotiation. You can conduct an online salary search (try *http://www.salary.com*) to help inform you of pay ranges by job and geographic area. You might also ask current employees of the company for their input.

If you are going for a position that includes incentives, learn about the total package, including those incentives and opportunities for stock options and bonuses. Try to discern how likely it is that you will reach the highest level of the compensation package. In other words, ask for historical data on average total compensation paid as a percentage of the potential. If the total number is $75,000 but 25 percent is tied to incentives, you need to know how much of that 25 percent you can reasonably count on for your own cash flow. Are the goals to reach incentives realistic? Are objectives adjusted during the year if a major change in economy, business sector, or supply and demand occurs? Can those goals be adjusted downward as well as upward?

If you want this job and the offer is lower than you'd hoped for, ask for a higher number as long as it is within reason.

> *If the job offer is lower than you'd hoped, decide how much the difference means to your life and if it's worth passing on a job that could give you real long-term growth potential and day-to-day satisfaction.*

Decide how much the difference means to your life and if it's worth passing on a job that could give you real long-term growth potential and day-to-day satisfaction. Other options are to ask if a six-month review is possible, what the raise history is (percentage), and if it's possible for you to earn more than that historical percentage if you prove to be the winner you believe you are. Ask about raises through promotion and if the opportunity for large percentage jumps in compensation occurs within the company.

If compensation is the currency of respect in your business, be sure to negotiate a dignified number for yourself. You have to feel good about the money so that you aren't bogged down with a nagging negative feeling that will hinder your energy toward your work. You want to be free of all encumbrances so that you can concentrate on great work.

Contracts are another two-sided issue. People's opinions vary vastly on this subject. The spectrum goes from enjoying the added security benefit to feeling as if you are handcuffing yourself to a place before you're sure if you like it or want to stay there. The length of the contract and the state of the job market will probably make a difference in how you feel. A contract that lasts only one year is a no-brainer because it will take you that long to learn how much you will enjoy the place. Two years might not be too long because a job search could take the better half of the second year if you decide you'd like to work elsewhere. Your feelings are personal, but the choice to sign a contract might not always be yours.

Understand the terms outright: What is the length of the contract? Are raises built in? Can the percentages change upward or downward? Is there a no-compete clause in the contract? What is the duration of the no-compete clause? (A no-compete clause means that you cannot work for a competitor in your field for a stipulated period of time.) Know exactly which companies are considered competitors, as well as which industries might be viewed as such and what the geographic limitations are. If you are not able to work in the field that you know, and are known in, try to negotiate an exit compensation package that will carry you for one-and-a-half to two times the duration of the no-compete clause. You could start your job search immediately, but if your no-compete restriction lasts for one year it will be almost impossible to be hired unless the new employer is willing to buy out the contract. Some companies will not even interview a person under a competing contract. Asking for two times the number of months you will be unable to work in your field will most likely carry you through until you can gain employment with a little left over. Remember that you'll have to keep your contacts up during this time and lunches, transportation, and presentations cost money.

Also know what the cycle for renewing the contract is. Are you given notice if your contract is not going to be renewed? Is nonrenewal a signal that you are no longer valuable to the company?

Contracts are good because they offer you stability and some security, but remember that contracts are always written for the company. Contracts are a tool for retaining talent or keeping talent from the competition even if their use to the current company is no longer deemed essential.

I never felt comfortable with the notion of a contract, in keeping with my own need to feel free. I wanted the option of knowing that I came to work each day because I wanted to be there. I did not want to be stuck at a place if people or policy changed hands and were no longer palatable to me. I was, however, once in a position to decline a contract because of my years of service and track within the company, as well as my level and value to the company. I made my position clear and offered my word to stay the minimum amount of time they deemed necessary to deliver the objectives, also making it clear that I loved the company and had no desire to leave. I wanted an open forum for discussions concerning raises and other aspects of my compensation. I also did not believe that signing a no-compete clause could ever be in my best interest.

Contracts are good because they offer you stability and some security, but remember that contracts are always written for the company. Declining to sign a contract can become a serious political issue if the company reads your hesitation as a sign of questionable loyalty.

Declining to sign a contract can become a serious political issue if the company reads your hesitation as a sign of questionable loyalty. It is incumbent on you to be very clear and sincere in your desire to serve the company well and long. It is also critical that you discern that the benefits under contract will still be yours (i.e., raises, options, exit package). You can achieve these advantages without signing a contract; remember that the company wants you to sign one because they want to keep you.

There might be places and stages when you have no option but to sign a contract if you want the job. There are some fields or companies for which signing a contract is standard hiring procedure. If you are joining a training program the company will want insurance that you will be on hand to deliver on that training. If the company is a startup and you are a partner or manager and your company is involved in venture capital funding, you are deemed an essential person that investors want to see in place. The funding could be in question if you are not under contract and your company (including your job and any option payoff) could be in jeopardy if investments don't come through.

QUESTIONS

- How does the company look and feel to you?

- How does the interviewer interact with you and others?

- Do you like the person you would be reporting to and do you think you could form a great working team?

- Are you satisfied with the mission statement, upward mobility, and opportunities for learning?

- Is this manager smart, passionate, and well connected within the company?

- Did you have the opportunity to have every question on your mind answered?

- Are you impressed with the questions the hiring manager asked of you?

- Are you comfortable with the compensation? Are you clear on incentives and how reachable the goals are?

- Do you care about contracts or not?

- Is the job a great enough opportunity that landing it transcends your concerns about money or contracts?

17 How to Pick (and Get Along With) Your Boss

Whenever you have an opportunity for a job change, you have the chance to carefully decide whom your next business leader and career guide will be. No one in your day-to-day work is more important than your immediate manager, because this person can help you to learn and grow, while building an environment where real happiness and fulfillment in the workplace are possible. Contrarily, a bad boss can make your entire life absolutely miserable.

You hopefully know what motivates and inspires you, and you have some idea of the long-term career path you'd like to take. You know the communication style that works best for you, and you also know the values that you bring to the party and want to live and work by. When you and your leadership are in sync in terms of values, communication, intent, politics, and process, you can be most free to enjoy and deliver excellent and fulfilling work.

> *When you and your leadership are in sync in terms of values, communication, intent, politics, and process, you can be most free to enjoy and deliver excellent and fulfilling work.*

Your manager is your most important contact for as long as you stay and he or she is in place, and possibly as long as you both grow with the company. A great manager can help you stretch and be the best possible you. You will break barriers and think in new ways and learn a lot about managing from a great one. Your manager should encourage, teach, and advocate for you and you might even move up the career ladder together.

If you work for an incompetent manager, your life can be difficult and distressed. If you have a bully boss you might be scathed; an autocrat might silence you; a micromanager might just drive you crazy. If he or she is not well thought of in the company and you are known as his or her "person," the negative connotation might rub off on you. If you are an idealist working for a realist you might feel thwarted, whereas a realist working for an idealist might find frustration.

Your value as a contributor gives you the right to be careful and selective about the people you give your talent to. I can't stress enough how important it is to have a talented, enlightened, compatible, and generous leader in front of you.

You are either interviewing as an internal candidate or fresh from the outside, perhaps with reference help from a current employee. If you are external, your homework is obvious. Check the company Web site, including the latest annual report. Ask your customers or vendors about the company to gain an outside perspective. If you know people in the company, ask questions about environment, leadership, and how realistic the goals are. Ask about the opportunities for upward mobility. If you are a minority, learn as much as you can about the company's policies and acceptance and advancement records.

Sometimes a person can be great manager for one group and a total nightmare for another. While you investigate during the interview, realize that your well-thought-out questions can become your competitive advantage.

Ask questions about the specific people you will be working with and for so that you can learn as much as possible about style, intellect, challenge, integrity, and environment. Ask a diverse group of people for references as well. Ask men, women, minorities, young starters, and the more experienced. Sometimes a person can be great manager for one group and a total nightmare for another. Although you might be treated well, being witness to shameful behavior is stressful for everyone and it will affect your environment.

If you are an internal candidate, your homework has been ongoing. You know the different parts of the company, who the great leaders are, what is produced, and which objectives have been met with outstanding results. You will also know how this job opportunity fits into the overall long-term scheme you have created for yourself.

Learning about the pressures on the manager, and the style in which he or she works and handles stress, will go a long way toward informing you how well you match. Compatibility is important and portends well for your happiness, productivity, and growth. While you investigate during the interview, realize that your well-thought-out questions can become your competitive advantage. Interviewing an intelligent, aware, energetic, strategic-minded individual really excites a hiring manager. Let your questions portray the way you think.

There will be times, as in a company takeover or internal movement, that you will inherit a new leader and then your job will be to start the new relationship on a positive note. Take your new manager's lead in order to learn and adapt. No matter what you might have heard about this person, try hard to take an "innocent until proven guilty" approach. Ask about your new leader's background, skills, and current agenda for your area.

Chances are the new manager will be filled in about you and your colleagues from previous management, human resources, or outside sources such as customers. Your new boss might also invite you to a meeting for an introductory session. Take such an opportunity to listen well and prepare a question list for all the areas you'd like covered. This is also a great time to be yourself and let this person know who you are and what you offer as a person as well as a worker. If you want to be sure you're counted as an important part of the team, state this. It is your responsibility to discover as much as possible about your compatibility, as well as any new goals or change that this new leader might bring to the place.

Interviewing an intelligent, aware, energetic, strategic-minded individual really excites a hiring manager. Let your questions portray the way you think and become your competitive advantage.

Bring the self-knowledge regarding your value with you on your interviews as you discover the needs of your prospective manager and the business at hand. What are the immediate objectives of the unit? What pressures surround the unit? What are the overall objectives of the larger company and how does your division fit in? It is important to understand the pressure your boss will have to live with so that you can keep your expectations in the proper realm. This understanding and your estimation of how well you will fit ultimately serve your own goals of career growth, fulfillment and purpose. You will also be able to surmise how you can raise your value to this person.

RULES FOR SUCCESSFUL INTERVIEWING AND FOLLOW-UP

- Always call to confirm the appointment.
- Ask for the job.
- Ask how you should proceed.
- Reiterate any follow-up.
- Always follow up with a letter of thanks to the person for their time, thought, and input.
- Always include your primary contact, the hiring manager, in any follow-up with a simple cc on any correspondence.

First things first, however. Always call to confirm the appointment. This shows that you are "buttoned up" and have respect for the busy life this person leads. Ask for the job. Let the hiring manager see that you're not afraid to go for the close. Reiterate any follow-up. Perhaps you were asked for references or a presentation; ask for due dates. Ask how you should proceed. Should you call in a few days or the following week? Would this person prefer to call you? If you are asked to wait for a call, this can feel tricky if too much time lapses. Give it four or five business days and then log a call to the office telling his or her assistant or voice mail that you are just checking in. You don't want to be a pest, and you want to prove that you listen well, but you want to express your keen interest and stay on the radar screen. Gauge what you can about this person's openness to your eagerness, because too many calls can be a turn off. Always follow up with a letter of thanks to the person for their time, thought, and input. Reiterate any of the strong points you agreed on and reiterate your strong interest in the position. Further follow-up might include an interview with one or more people that you will be interacting with in your new post. Always include your primary contact, the hiring manager, in any follow-up with a simple copy on any correspondence. This saves phone calls, time, and any awkwardness for all involved.

The interview is a time of investigation for both parties. There is a lot to learn about the employer through simple and relaxed actions and interactions. Look for personality and character clues throughout every meeting.

- Is the interviewer courteous to the people he or she interacts with?
- Does he or she seem to treat men, women, and minorities the same?
- Is the style professional and the same with each group, or do you detect flirtation or disdain with a member of the opposite sex or a minority?
- If you are at a restaurant pay close attention to manners in general and how this person treats the wait staff. What sort of tip does your host leave? Is this person generous or greedy, mannered or not?
- Is this person's desk clean or cluttered? What does either say to you?
- How comfortably and often are you getting eye contact?
- Is he or she double tasking, such as looking at the computer monitor for incoming e-mails? Is this an indication of boredom with your interview, or does this person have a short attention span?
- How would these indicators translate into your day-to-day interactions and comfort level?
- See if the style is consistent in subsequent meetings and always observe the person and the surroundings.

Once I was interviewing candidates for a position and I asked the three finalists to come in for a meeting with my boss. While one person waited in the lobby outside of his office, she was able to hear this man screaming at his wife on the telephone. She was aghast and she got some idea of what this man might be about. I was completely embarrassed after selling this bright person on what a great company this was to join.

- *Communication style*—Direct or vague? Clear, precise, appropriate, inclusive, or gossipy? Blunt or tactful? Verbal, written, e-mail, meetings, informal and often, or formal and structured? Does this person give feedback often or only when asked? Is there an open-door policy or are meetings by appointment only? Are competency reviews held annually or more often? Can you ask for progress updates as you need them?

- *Management style*—Will this person delegate or micromanage? Consensus builder or autocrat? Exclusive or inclusive? Generous in attribution or a greedy credit-taker? Are you hearing a lot of "I" as opposed to "we?" Is this manager a teacher with champion possibilities? Will he or she back you if you are down? Will this manager take the heat from above and push it down, or will he or she stand up and harbor the team when it is appropriate to do so? Is he or she a team builder? Does he or she enjoy pushback (freedom to disagree vs. autocracy)? How important is process? Is this person an innovator or a reactor? Is a new idea exciting no matter who generates it, or is it irritating if it wasn't his or her proposition? Is this leader a change agent or a protector of the status quo?

- *Needs*—What keeps him or her up at night? What's missing from the team and how can you fill the gap? What are the goals of this area? How reachable are they? What are the current hurdles? How do the objectives affect compensation (without getting into detail about your salary level until a later interview)? What are the required competencies of the post you are interviewing for? If this is an inherited manager, have the competency requirements changed?

- *Background*—Where has this person been? What are the future goal destinations? This is important and will give you many clues. If this is a person who is very happy in the current post and doesn't plan to move, your growth in this area might be blocked or stalled. This might require you to make a move to another location in the company or geographic area, or even leave the company. If this manager is on a fast track, how much longer does he or she expect to be in this post and who is the heir apparent? This information will help you make an informed decision and give you an eye on the near and long-term future.

- *Energy level*—Does the manager's energy seem to match yours? Is he or she up and quick and smart and pleasant? Does this person laugh easily and smile often or is his or her style more fidgety, nervous, and uncomfortable? Is this person slow and methodical or a fast-paced multitasker?

- *Championship material*—Try to glean the respect this person has internally, from every angle possible. Ask where past direct reports are today. Look for clues in the office from award plaques or event pictures: Who else is in them? Does this person have a champion? Who is the champion and how well connected is that person? Does he or she believe in championing a protégé? Will this manager be open to conversations with you about your growth, advocate for you, and brainstorm with you on new ideas?

- *What's the motivator*—Challenge? Winning? Reaching goals? Money? Promotion? Power? Learn what parts of the job are most exciting and most tedious for this individual.

Make your own list of questions for the interview. Keep them in hand and save them for the question-and-answer period at the end of the interview. Throughout, see how many issues you can intertwine into the conversation so that you can glean answers without having to ask.

I was once in a series of interviews for a high-level job. The first meeting found me answering all the questions. The second meeting, by the hiring manager's invitation, was reserved for all my questions. I knew I wanted to work for this person simply because he gave me the forum to be clear about his objectives and the company in total. He was also able to learn a lot about me from my questions. The result was four wonderful years of building, growth, learning, and achieving because we were in sync. In retrospect these might have been the best years of my working life, and we even had some rough times. This man was a listener and an enlightened manager. We chose each other wisely.

QUESTIONS

- How can you enhance your interview investigation?

- What areas and subsequent questions should you add to those listed throughout this chapter?

18 MANAGEMENT BY TYPE

Whether you select or inherit your boss, you'll be in a better position to manage your success by understanding that person well. Let's profile the perfect boss based on competencies that you've decided work well with you. The leader is open minded, decisive, fair yet firm, inclusive, brilliant, passionate and optimistic, while supplying opportunities for learning, winning, growth, and advancement.

Favorite managers have open-door policies, provide feedback on a timely basis, care about your money and your life, and never have a bad day. They don't gossip, they don't lose their tempers, they're evenhanded, and they can handle a great deal of stress without exploding or passing it down to the people who work directly for them. Your boss cares about the environment, is empathic, wants your feedback on policy, and loves to give attribution.

Okay, even if every manager in the world strives to be as good as this, nobody is perfect. As long as we see the major good points, we can probably live with a few bad ones. The critical competencies that you want in a manager might come down to intelligence, integrity, fairness, decisiveness, mentorship, and good, clear, honest communication. You want your manager to be well thought of within the company and well connected. You want your manager to have a voice with the high-level executives in the organization and for the work in your department to be highly respected and important to the company.

The following is a review of some types of managers and recommendations on how you can navigate your way to a successful relationship with them.

MEN VERSUS WOMEN AS MANAGERS

Leaders have competencies that transcend gender. People have styles that differentiate them from one another. Intelligence, passion, strategic thinking, and open-mindedness have no gender. You can work for someone who is a confident, intelligent, generous mentor without gender being an issue. You can have a bully boss, an insecure one, or an egotistical one that is either a man or a woman. A person can be exclusionary or inclusive regardless of gender. Stereotypes in terms of style still abound.

Intelligence, passion, strategic thinking, and open-mindedness have no gender. Greatness, or lack of it, is about the person's viewpoint, intelligence and passion, style, experience, and contacts in and outside of the company.

Men are thought to be the most aggressive and women are still tagged as being catty. There are plenty of aggressive women and plenty of catty men.

A U.S. Census Bureau survey released in March 2003 found that 9.4 million women worked in executive or managerial positions, accounting for 45 percent of such jobs in 2002. As genders and styles blend, competencies will lead and stereotypes about both genders might further evaporate.

To reiterate, competencies, high-level internal connections, and your comfort level with the person are what matter most in terms of evaluating a leader. It is important to know if this person is regarded as a player in the company, is championed, if people enjoy working for him or her, and if he or she has personal champion potential for you. It would be helpful to know how this person has related to and promoted members of the opposite sex because you want to work for a person who is aware, enlightened, and egalitarian.

I've worked for great women and not-so-great women. I've worked for great men and not-so-great men. Greatness, or lack of it, is about the person's viewpoint, intelligence and passion, style, experience, and contacts in and outside of the company. People are people with their own sets of skills, goals, needs, and likes. It is your job to discern how best you fit with their style.

INNIES VERSUS OUTIES AS MANAGERS

Remember back to your adolescent and teenage days when popularity and peer pressure were major sources of stress? We had our leaders, sports heroes, cheerleaders, and excellent students. We also had the wannabes. A yesterday wannabe doesn't easily shed that suit. If you are working for a person who has something to prove to the world, much less to himself or herself, it might not be an easy ride for you as a subordinate. In other words, a person with a lot to prove sometimes lacks confidence and the manifested insecurity shows in many ways. You could encounter stinginess when it comes to contacts or information, because knowledge is power. You might not receive proper attribution because the outie needs the kudos. You might feel oppressed rather than free because the insecure manager is likely to draw a strict territorial line you cannot cross. This means you'll have to run absolutely everything through this type of boss and he or she will use veto power freely to maintain complete control. This manager is likely to be intimidated if you ask for champion mentoring or come up with an idea that crosses into other departments. It's most likely a jealousy thing: This person needs to be the best and the brightest. The outie needs to matter and to succeed very much, very deeply.

This person needs to be the best and the brightest. The outie needs to matter and to succeed very much, very deeply.

If you work for someone who has "outie baggage" you have some recourse. Work within the rules and help solidify his or her confidence so that you will be free to produce creatively. Become a kingmaker so the edge can soften between you, and perhaps even move the person up and out of your way. Work with this person with loads of empathy if you can muster it. Become the best possible go-to person by being responsible, accountable, and most of all, trustworthy. Humility on your part counts to the outie. Little by little, you'll get to do more. Outies aren't necessarily selfish people; they're just needy, and that has its effects.

THE BULLY BOSS

The bully boss leaves many people tired, distressed, and in a quandary. Bully bosses are my least favorite type of person to work with or for. A blustery boss is actually not as effective as the generated noise level would have you think. Ignorant behavior is very expensive to a company, and it is hard to accept that this type of person can be called a leader and often defended, protected, and even promoted.

When bully managers win through intimidation, they get to direct the action as they see it without challenge. This also means the bully boss has to be incredibly smart and prescient because he or she works without consensus or feedback the majority of the time. What do bully managers miss? They miss ideas, loyalty and truth. They quash enthusiasm and entrepreneurial spirit. Bully bosses cost the company money in misplaced energy, lawsuits, loss of important players, and ramp-up costs for new employees. Intimidating managers believe they are all-powerful because people quake in their wake. These leaders miss respect and the opportunity for personal and team growth.

Bully bosses certainly cost businesses money in mental and physical health costs and in productivity due to days missed. Most businesses today conduct diversity-training classes so employees can better understand the laws and the company policies regarding behavior toward others around them, especially those who are different from themselves. The classes are also meant to encourage leaders to embrace thoughts from groups that might shed new light on an old situation through different viewpoints. Companies hold seminars that take people away from their work for hours in the hope of avoiding lawsuits and enlightening their employees, but many problem people are not fired.

In my experience, most bullies have some degree of proving to do, but do they really win in the long run? They are likely to miss the next big idea or find an expensive error because people are afraid to speak up, or because people don't want to make those managers look good.

Why are these people allowed to continue acting out in harmful ways? One reason is that most people are too intimidated to report incidents to human resources. Another reason is that people see the consistent promotions of bully bosses and realize that policy be damned: If the person achieves superb results, negative behavior is not always seriously reprimanded.

If you find yourself working for a bully boss, you are likely to lose sleep unless you are completely inured to rude and hurtful behavior. If you are unfazed by someone screaming at you, then I'd say you have either a very tough skin or you have been abused and have come to expect it. You might even be like the person in the first place. If you are a bully boss, do your best to see the damage you cause and the ideas and opportunities for improvement that you might miss. There are humane ways to accomplish tough goals and still be a king.

> *Bully bosses are likely to miss the next big idea or find an expensive error because people are afraid to speak up, or because people don't want to make those managers look good.*

I worked for a couple of bully bosses and I was in the company of others who I, thankfully, did not report to. I found this behavior to be repugnant and I never got used to it or accepted it. I usually confronted the bully boss head on and explained what I thought about the behavior and how I wanted to be treated. This would surprise them even if it didn't totally change them. At least it seemed to calm them down. Although I took going to HR to complain very seriously, I did this at least twice in my career. In those cases I did not necessarily want to harm the person's career; I simply wanted to have a good place to work.

If I spotted rude, bully behavior among people that reported to me, I called them on it immediately. There have been times when I brought people together to discuss the ramifications of the behavior on the bully and the trampled. I gave the bully a chance to apologize and the trampled a chance to let the offender know what it felt like. Slowly but surely we saw improvement.

I suggest that in most cases you muster the courage to confront the bully boss face to face first. Ask for an appointment at a calm time and plan your approach. Honesty is disarming if the tone and language used are sincere and kind. Let the person know how tyranny affects you and reflects on him or her. Speak as a helpful associate rather than an angry employee. I once opened such a conversation by stating that I took responsibility for our relationship not always working and I wanted to discuss our communication style. I then went on to let the person know that yelling didn't motivate me in a positive way: "I want to be a contributing and positive part of your team, but these outbursts kill my enthusiasm and crush my morale and that of others." Our relationship improved markedly. I also learned when to stay away by gauging mood and behavior. A meeting late, but well timed, is better than one when the bully boss is in a hungry mood.

> *A meeting late, but well timed, is better than one when the bully boss is in a hungry mood. There is no badge of honor in living through hell and helping a tyrant reach new heights.*

If nothing changes after time and you are feeling abused, go to human resources and file a complaint against the person. If the person who is upsetting you and your environment is a known tyrant and if you are indeed afraid of recrimination from this person, skip the one-on-one meeting and go right to HR. I knew of one most despicable bully who was known to make even men cry. This serious bully was simply a bad guy, and going directly to this sort of person will get you nothing but further trampled.

If you are uncomfortable filing a formal complaint, at least take action verbally. If the person does happen to be brilliant and brings in impressive results, it is possible that the charge will not see the light of day. In too many cases, these people will be promoted out before they are displaced entirely from the company. Still, do not let this stop you from going forward. The company needs to know about the inappropriate behavior and they need to know that you are at risk.

If the situation is continuous and prolonged, with no hope for change, ask for a transfer to another department or team or get your plan B together to prepare to leave. Don't let your departure inform your feelings, in a negative way, about yourself. It will be the company's loss whether they see it now or not. There is no badge of honor in living through hell and helping a tyrant reach new heights. The bully boss can do it on his or her own and probably will. Your misery is likely to rub off on your personal relationships and on your mental and physical health. Living through hell doesn't win you a badge for being tough, but it might win you a prescription for antidepressants.

IDEALISTS VERSUS REALISTS

Idealists visualize things or situations as they believe they should be rather than as they are. They are passionate in their beliefs and spend energy rallying those around them to see the vision and to work toward the goal. These people are usually optimistic and resilient, and they question and push. They are tenacious and sincere in their beliefs and they have a great deal of willpower. If they are also charismatic they can be leaders that ignite energies and offer a great deal of purpose and meaning to the employees. Idealists stretch boundaries and bend rules, with integrity, to expand minds and achieve results along the way. Idealists don't understand the word "no" and go for the best possible scenario rather than just an outcome that is good enough. They can be a nuisance to constituents who are not like them, and they might feel very constricted working for a realist manager. The idealist is motivated by a vision of the greater win, is usually inclusive, and understands that success on the larger scale will mean success for him or her as well. Entrepreneurs are often idealists: Think of Jeff Bezos of Amazon.com or Bill Gates of Microsoft. Change agents are often idealists.

The realist sees things as they are, or as they believe the rules dictate. Realists might understand the benefits of a new action or goal, but they can also see the hurdles. Realists are more likely to avoid assignments or take on new projects if they believe they will be politically, or otherwise, difficult to execute.

Realists work within the lines to deliver a goal. They accept the rules and the standards and execute the plan. They are good subordinates in that they don't rock the boss's boat. They get things done, usually correctly and on time. They are driven to deliver the stated goals and they have the ability to see the big picture. The realist understands and wants to achieve great things for the company and is often more ego-driven and territorial than the idealist. He or she is also likely to be less sensitive in general and more thick-skinned about politics and able to navigate a winning road without turmoil or great change.

As managers, idealists want to be surrounded by people who are thinkers and those who push back, stretch, and even insist that creativity, environment, and consensus are the constitution of a great workplace. More often than not, the realist manager wants people who accept their direction as dogma and execute without question or controversy. They don't want to waste time straying from the prescribed recipe. Their goal is superb results for the task at hand. Often, realists are less likely to be consensus builders than idealists. The realist understands and encourages chain-of-command politics. They can question but do not expect to be questioned. Just give them the work they ask for and don't present any problems or forks in the road.

If you are an idealist working for a realist you could have some difficulty if you find that your creativity is stifled on a regular basis. You must adapt to your boss's way of thinking and execution so that you'll be in his or her good graces and prove yourself to be a valuable member of the team. If this is difficult for you, you might try to strike a deal with the realist boss. Ask if you can submit additional ideas on the side. You will listen and react to the realist's wishes and be part of the execution team; if he or she is willing to hear new or expanded ideas, you can still be you. The sell to this person is that you might have an idea that makes a great deal of sense and will make him or her look even better to the high-level managers in the company.

> If you are an idealist working for a realist you could have some difficulty if you find that your creativity is stifled on a regular basis. If you are a realist working for an idealist, you might become frustrated or impatient with a process that doesn't suit the analytical side of your brain.

If you are a realist working for an idealist, you might become frustrated or impatient with a process that doesn't suit the analytical side of your brain. You might be asked to come up with ideas beyond the stated goal and you'll wonder why you have to do more or different work than what is asked for. If this is the case, try to get into the game. Try to understand why your boss works this way and discover the merits of it. Look for evidence of historical success within this idealist's format. You might come to enjoy the out-of-the-box thinking, or you might fortify your own realist belief and behavior. At the very least you will quickly learn who you are and seek a better match on your next move.

By determining if you and your boss are idealists or realists, you will better understand the culture and the expectations of the place and whether you are a fit. My own belief is that idealists do a great deal of good to any organization. They challenge the status quo, rally passionately and energetically, and get people to think. In essence, their innate being raises the standards of the unit they manage. Depending on the tenor of the place, however, the realist might have the advantage because of specific needs or timing. There is something seductive about a person who "gets it" from the boss's point of view.

Realists offer no problems because they don't question directives, even if they might have a better idea.

My experience is that idealists push the standards and boundaries, but realists get the objectives completed most efficiently. If you don't ask questions, push the envelope or gain consensus, your trip from A to B is much faster. Expedience isn't always best, but it counts for a great deal in the analytical, accountable world of Wall Street that we live in today. There is also no measure for what might have been, so there is no real proof of one type's advantage over the other.

There is room and need for both types of managers. The company needs and the working style of the highest-level managers will decide which type will rise up. After you identify whether you are a realist or an idealist, you might want to search for companies or types of businesses that lead with this characteristic. Idealists and realists don't have to be polar opposites. The optimum is to strive to be a bit of both and this is the rare and special leader. Stretch, create, visualize, and mobilize, keeping timelines and budgets in view and on point.

THE EGOMANIAC

This person is usually easy to spot, as the use of "I" or "My" is incessant: My people, my team, my idea, my stock price, my, my, my . . . me, me, me. Everything is about, or in service of, this person. This type of manager hoards credit, information, contacts, and ideas because he or she believes knowledge is power and it is not to be shared. These managers take credit for other people's ideas and give little or no attribution for contributions from others. They respond to sycophants and surround themselves with adoring fans, creating a "clubby" atmosphere in which they can exclude others to feel important. They also build walls so that no one with a different idea can permeate their defenses.

One way to work for a narcissistic egomaniac is to try to accept the person for exactly what he or she is and hope that he or she will get promoted or moved up and out of your way soon. You might feel oppressed and stifled working for this type of person, or very bored with the self-adulation. Try to remember that the problems that ensue are probably not about you. It is very unsettling to make contributions that remain anonymous or are ignored because of someone else's ego needs. This happens many times in any career and the most egregious cases might even cause you to seek employment elsewhere. If you feel hidden and used you might find, after a time, that you lose the motivation to continue providing game-changing suggestions to this type of manager. You might actually need to be creative and innovative, and you do not want to be hidden. These are difficult desires to have if you are working for someone whose foot is on your face. All does not have to be lost. There is a place between changing who you are and finding a new job.

Copy other people on important, game-changing suggestions. Invite other leaders, including yours, to client gatherings. Be prepared for all meetings so that your work will be showcased to a wider group. Stay close to your mentor-champion and keep him or her up to date on your contributions.

Being a kingmaker is one thing; being a foolish kingmaker is another. Why help this person reach his or her level of incompetence? The leader is the person who creates the environment where people stretch and think and act out of the norm for the betterment of the company . . . or not.

THE ONE WITH TWO FACES

This type of manager makes you feel as if you are the only person in the room. Your input matters a great deal, and you receive smiles and nods of agreement and encouragement. Once you leave the room, however, you'll be talked about to colleagues and management in a negative way that you would never ascribe to him or her. You wouldn't think it true or possible, but it is. Managers with two faces are out for themselves beyond any other objective. They will motivate you to get the desired work needed to cement a good personal perception from their own bosses for themselves. The one with two faces is a sycophant who manages up very well and won't mind cutting you out of the way if doing so helps his or her own upward mobility. Look out.

What can you do if you're working for a two-faced manager? Deliver stellar work, on time, every time. Engage in business conversations but never gossip. This person is not your friend, so don't be fooled or taken in by flowing charms. Don't give this person any reason to speak ill of you, as far as you can control it. Listen well to make sure you're right about your perception of this person's character; and if you learn that you have been spoken of in a way that is not true or fair, find a way to confront him or her about it directly. Speak in nonemotional terms with this type of manager while continuing to be a positive influence on your team or work unit.

> *Managers with two faces are out for themselves beyond any other objective. They will motivate you to get the desired work needed to cement a good personal perception from their own bosses for themselves.*

THE CHARMING MONSTER

The charming monster is a close cousin to the one with two faces and has the genetic code of the bully boss, albeit more dormant. The only real difference is that this type of manager doesn't care what you think about him or her. The charming monster talks about people behind their backs and confronts them to their faces. This person is ultraconfident and aggressive and pushes his or her own personal agenda to the mat. The charming monster will nod to the boss and do what he or she wants to anyway. This type of manager is very good at being exclusive and autocratic, and wears the power suit well. The charming monster is exceedingly competitive, egotistical, and fearless, but here's the rub: The charming monster can build a loyal constituency. He or she is a winner, even if you don't always like the way the win is achieved.

If you work for a charming monster, try to pick the time that you address him or her so that you get to work with the charming persona instead of the monster one. If you are going to disagree with the charming monster, you must do it deferentially or the monster might come out. If the charming monster thinks you are a threat, look out, because you might be bullied, gossiped about, or excluded.

This is my second least favorite type of boss after the bully boss because charming monsters have a childlike quality about them that helps them get away with a lot. Like an older brother or sister, they beat up on a sibling and repeat over and over to their parents that they didn't do it. It is rare that the manager of the charming monster ever sees him or her act badly. Be buttoned up, be friendly, and don't worry about what this type of person has to say to or about you, because the charming monster cannot be controlled. Continue delivering excellent work; just be sure not to be fooled by the charm.

> *The charming monster talks about people behind their backs and confronts them to their faces. This person is ultraconfident and aggressive and pushes his or her own personal agenda to the mat.*

The theme that underlines success with any type of boss is your own excellence. Great work delivered in the manner requested and on time trumps type. Don't be afraid to take action if it is called for, or to stand up for yourself if you need to. Exposing bad seeds in a good company might get you the results you hope for.

QUESTIONS

- What attributes do you want in the person you report to?

- Which undesirable traits can you live with?

- How can you best discover the manager's type and style?

- Who can you ask for honest references on the person?

- How compatible are you with your current boss?

- Is this person's unit making objectives?

- Is this person's unit happy, fulfilled, and empowered?

- Can you identify core values that you have in common or the opposite: Are the values that are important to you at odds with this type of person?

- What steps can you take for better compatibility with a manager you don't respect or like?

- Will you attempt to correct the relationship by speaking directly with the person?

- Is the problem with a bad boss important enough for you to consider leaving a company you otherwise admire?

19 PREPARING FOR YOUR ANNUAL REVIEW: MANAGING YOUR VALUE PERCEPTION

Most companies conduct annual reviews to keep you and your management in sync regarding perception and growth. The time spent will inform you about the current level of recognition of your work, offer a discussion about your future, and reflect any changes in compensation. Although there might be opportunities throughout the year for casual mentoring with your management, the annual review will go into your file; it is important and will speak about you to people you don't know personally. The review might be pulled if you are under consideration for a promotion, if you have a change in management, or if you are in a trouble spot with your management. Time and consideration before the meeting will go a long way toward assisting your own advocacy efforts.

> The annual review will go into your file; it is important and will speak about you to people you don't know personally. The review might be pulled if you are under consideration for a promotion, if you have a change in management, or if you are in a trouble spot with your management.

Preparation for this meeting is essential. Take the time to review the competency evaluation form that will be filled out by your management and take an objective view of your contributions and shortfalls. Fill out the form with answers from your manager's viewpoint if you can. You might already know what skills and perceptions you want to improve. After you look through your manager's eyes, fill it out again as you'd like to see it finalized and begin to build an honest case for each line that might need and deserve strengthening. By seeing your strengths and areas for improvement on your own you will be better prepared to ask for help that will ensure your growth. You will also impress your management with the commitment you bring to the evaluation process.

> *By seeing your strengths and areas for improvement on your own you will be better prepared to ask for help that will ensure your growth.*

Outline the areas you'd like discussed and construct exhibits for each one. These might take the form of five separate one-sheet outlines or memos.

1. Contributions since the last review.
2. Strong-suit competencies that apply to current and future positions.
3. Areas you'd like to improve on.
4. Responsibilities you'd like to grow into.
5. A schema describing your vision of your future with the company.

It is fine to go beyond the confines of the printed review form so that your important issues are covered, but be aware of the time constraints on your meeting. If you need more time, ask for it at the appropriate place in the evaluation meeting. The one-sheet exhibits will keep your discussion on track and timely, and they might also prove to be a defense against a rating you don't agree with.

CONTRIBUTIONS SINCE THE LAST REVIEW

Prepare a one-sheet that outlines your contributions since your last review. Think about each aspect of your job and have proof of your success as backup in case you need it. If you've been keeping a file of significant actions your preparation task will be that much easier.

For the one-sheet presentation, outline your success and important wins: (e.g., sales or other numerical achievements), new business development, new product introductions, managing change, aiding (new) management, rethinking and improving old processes, or positioning a product that resulted in price increases. Include any other tangible improvement that you shepherded for your specific area. Bring proof of your work that aided the company in reaching its profit goals. This would include making budgets, prudent cost reductions, unit rate increases, production management, inventory sellout, positioning or repositioning a product to market, improving processes to reduce redundancy, winning an important customer for the company, recruiting, retaining and developing key players in the organization, and so on. Also be able to discuss your part in leadership and espousing the company ideals through team building, helping the team to remain focused and productive in spite of internal problems, or boosting morale for the unit internally and externally.

If you've been keeping a file of significant actions your preparation task will be that much easier.

STRONG-SUIT COMPETENCIES THAT APPLY TO CURRENT AND FUTURE POSITIONS

A separate sheet should identify and outline the competencies required for your current position and the one you'd like next. In addition to the skills listed on the evaluation form, discuss areas such as leadership, vision, product knowledge, customer relations, communication and mentoring, organizational skills, integrity, resourcefulness, task orientation, speed and accuracy, adaptability, analytical skills, and conflict resolution. You should consider and judge these areas for yourself first. Be honest so you know the areas that are your strong suits and those you'd like help with. Be prepared with two or three specific examples to prove your competency in each area, and be able to go deeper if asked.

AREAS YOU'D LIKE TO IMPROVE ON

To admit your areas of weakness is a strong show of courage and willingness to improve. Ask for help where you need it. Perhaps it is the internal political area, analytical or financial skills, diversity training, follow-up or time management, or process and planning. Take this opportunity to discuss company-sponsored training or adult education classes you might take to strengthen a designated skill set. Your willingness to improve yourself will be impressive. Identify your perceived shortfalls with your management and create a plan to work on these competencies within the next year, possibly asking for reviews on these sectors in six months. You might be surprised to learn that you are harder on yourself than your manager is. Take the win, but continue to strive to be more excellent in the areas in which you need improvement.

> *To admit your areas of weakness is a strong show of courage and willingness to learn. Letting your manager know you want to grow will put you in place faster than any other action.*

RESPONSIBILITIES YOU'D LIKE TO GROW INTO

Think about the parts of your job you most enjoy and see if you can identify a role or a need in the company that exploits those characteristics and competencies. Look at your sheet on strong suits and see where you might fit in best. Letting your management know you want to grow will put you in that place faster than any other action. This meeting is a communication about current and future status. Use it.

A SCHEMA DESCRIBING YOUR VISION OF YOUR FUTURE WITH THE COMPANY

This area goes beyond responsibilities you'd like to grow into because you are sharing your long-term vision with your management. It might be a bit intimidating for you to say that you want your boss's job or that you are interested in moving to another area in the company. If you are a strong employee your manager will be surprised if you didn't claim this aim.

It is not a bad thing to know the steps you want to take with your career and where you see yourself realistically topping out. You might want to be the CEO of the company, but is this a real possibility? What are the obstacles that you can see to the jobs you want to attain in the long term? How can you begin to prepare now to combat those hurdles? Which jobs will best prepare you on your road? What additional classes do you need to take? Who is the champion that can mentor you along the way? A candid conversation with your management or with human resources puts your vision on the map and on the record.

This analysis counts for many positive moves in your personal kingdom planning as well. You can judge timing in each position and also begin to gauge your career exit year. Maybe you'll want to start your own business one day. Learn as much as you can from your company to create your own future CEO post if that is your desire. When you have this vision in mind you can begin to build an action plan for your current career as well as your post-corporate life.

This analysis counts for many positive moves in your personal kingdom planning as well.

HOW TO DISAGREE WITH YOUR MANAGER'S VIEWPOINT

I always found that excellent people wanted and expected excellent reviews and were often taken aback when a "surprise" criticism came their way. If they got a rating of 3 instead of 4 they fought me and showed me where I might be wrong. I actually changed reviews on the spot in a few instances because I saw the sincerity and the proof and because I realized that the score was less important than having this person *believe* he or she was contributing in an important area. I would make a case for my perception, but include the employee's rebuttal in my reversal. The person would still think about the conversation and strive to improve the perception of the competency discussed.

I fought reviews twice in my career. The first was in the early stages when women in television sales were still scarce and my management believed that the big, handsome hunks should call on the major (mostly female) buyers. The other woman on the sales force and I were relegated to the tough shops with low budgets and business that our top-rated stations could live without. (Actually, our lessons learned equipped us well for television's future of more competition and more difficult negotiations.) I was marked low for "adaptability" because I was calling on buying services rather than the A list of advertising agencies. I challenged my boss that perhaps it was he who was not adaptable and that I should be given an opportunity to call on these agencies. He changed his mind, changed my score, and gave me a better customer list. This was an issue that he was blind to, but he was willing to change and I was able to grow and improve my value to that company and within the industry.

Another time I was grossly undervalued on my review. This was bitterly hurtful, as it was the first time in my management career that I had not been marked "ready for next position." In fact, the review basically said that I did not even fit the criteria for the position I held, after four years of superb reviews and a promotion to vice president. This was a case of new management who wanted to build its own leadership team. I argued that the review was unfair and asked for time to rebut each issue. In the end I decided to go to the mat for my good name and my contributions. I asked outright if this was an instrument to get rid of me and my manager weaseled out and said no. I perceived that the company needed me for another six months as they were downgrading other managers into sales positions and I would be used for stability and training the new management team. After a few sleepless nights I decided that I didn't see the positive return on investment for me in working with people I couldn't possibly trust. I also decided that I didn't want to be used for training the new people only to be possibly downgraded when they were in good shape. I wrote a rebuttal and delivered copies to my manager, the general manager, and human resources. I knew that if I took this action I had to be willing to leave the company and I was. I asked for a "divorce," spent a sunny month in Europe, practiced living in the "now," and landed a management job at a different TV station when I returned. It was treacherous and scary, but in the end it was all very, very good.

If you rebut an issue, be sure that you have your proof ready and ask that your manager hear you out. Ask for specific examples of instances in which you did not measure up to that certain competency and offer your rebuttal after he or she speaks. Decide if the battle is worth a war or if you can agree to disagree while giving your manager the respect of the leadership chair and vowing to work to improve the skill, or the perception of your skill, in the questioned area.

The annual raise in compensation is almost secondary to the information, even though the percentage increase vis à vis the company average will also tell you a lot about where you fit. If you are disappointed in the amount, say so, but do this only after some consideration. Negotiate if you feel you must, but do it gingerly in tough economic climates. When times are tough and you are getting a raise, try to be satisfied with the company average, thank profusely for more, and be very open to listening if your raise is below the middle point.

Use your annual review as an opportunity for learning about your boss, your relationship, and your perceived value and future in the organization. Prepare well and listen hard; this is the best place to learn about your career life in this company. Ask questions and don't be afraid to try to persuade the reviewer of a different view if you believe in it. There is no negative here. If you see that there is a gap in perception about your work and worth, you have the opportunity to change that view or set steps in motion that will turn it around.

QUESTIONS

- Will you create a file for significant contributions to make preparing for your annual review easier?

- Might this also prove to be convenient information for any impromptu controversies or conversations with your supermentor?

- Do you agree that value contributions or excellent results can be used as fodder for résumé updating?

- Will you give the five criteria in this chapter some thought and begin a worksheet for each one?

- How will this exercise inform you of actions you can take today?

- Will you start today?

20 KEEPING CLEAR ON WHAT YOU THINK YOU WANT

It is meaningful to your overall sense of fulfillment and happiness and to your ultimate success, that you understand why you want the next job or promotion, and what the opportunity risks are to your life in a whole sense.

What is driving you? Is it boredom in your current job and the belief that you can and want to do more? Are you in need of a new challenge and learning curve? Do you have a strong and passionate belief in the way things "should be" versus the current "as is"? How about money, ego, and power as motivators? Maybe you want to get away from your current manager or environment? There might be truth in the entire list, but which factors are leading you at this particular time in your life? The principal drivers will change as you change; it is valuable to stay "in tune" with yourself so that you are aware of what propels you.

> It is crucial that you understand your motivations and that you remain open to changes in the workplace and in your own perspective and value system, so that you don't make an ego-driven or otherwise shaky decision.

What are the risks? Do you have to relocate? Will it affect your business and personal relationships? Will it shrink your time for "other" life? What is the stress level? Who will you report to? How do you feel about that person? Will there be shifts in energy and focus, away from the work you love, to a new level of politics that might take you away from the work? Is there a security issue to the assignment; that is, are you filling a short-term need of the company with an open-ended future? Do you trust your management? How much are you willing to risk for the job that will take you to the position you really want? Will this next post keep you on your long-term goal path? Is there a significant jump in salary or benefits?

It is crucial that you understand your motivations and that you remain open to changes in the workplace and in your own perspective and value system, so that you don't make an ego-driven or otherwise shaky decision. Goals and perspectives will change as environments change and as you gain maturity and confidence. Finding time for introspection is essential to keeping in touch with yourself. Vacations are a great time to ask yourself some weighty questions. Where have you been? What has been most enjoyable? Which competencies or relationships do you need to work on? Where do you want your career to go next? How does this fit into your personal life and long-term, whole-life picture?

Some people start working on their next job the minute they get a new job. Why? Is this the cultural expectation in your workplace? Does it suit you? There is something wonderful about taking a position and working it until the priorities have been delivered. You will know when you are ready to move on. If your eye is always on tomorrow, how can you honestly excel to the fullest now? Enjoy where you are by exploiting every possible learning curve. New information about people, process, and product management only strengthens your future position. Sometimes it's just very nice to relax a bit and enjoy the fruits of your labor in a position that you've conquered. Moving up and on without a breather isn't always the only way to go. The key knowledge from every post will also serve to form your future goals with more clarity; you will know if you want to continue on your predesigned path or if goal changes are in order.

> *If your eye is always on tomorrow, how can you honestly excel to the fullest now? Sometimes it's just very nice to relax a bit and enjoy the fruits of your labor in a position that you've conquered.*

WHAT ARE YOU GETTING INTO?

It is very seductive and satisfying to be on an upward track within your organization. You feel acknowledged, "chosen," and important. You feel secure in your future and strong on confidence. You must beware and be aware of your personal needs, the needs of the company, and how they fit together. Sometimes ego blinds one to pitfalls that should be avoided in the long run. Sometimes you might move swiftly to embrace the new challenge, excited by the ego-satiating part of "being picked." It won't hurt to take a deep breath on the eve of new assignments and ask your prospective new managers and yourself some important questions.

Remember the company's ultimate goals: productivity, growth, profit, and stock price. Remember that you are a cog in the wheel and you are important as long as you are functional to these ends and you are trustworthy and comfortable to be with. Keep your own personal and professional goals foremost in your mind when you are making crucial decisions about your career. What is in it for you?

What are the benefits of this new job? Is this a growth or profit area for the company? Who will you report to? Who are the other members of the team? What new key learning will you acquire that you can't gain from your current post? Is this a more visible position? Will your work be exposed to the chief decision-makers in the company? Are the objectives accomplishable? Where will this job lead in two years? Will this job keep you on track or put you on the fast track to your ultimate goal? Might it sidetrack you while affording a learning opportunity that you want, or sideline you completely? Will the compensation propel your personal financial goals by any important measure? How much fun will you have?

How might this position enhance your résumé and make you more valuable in the company, and in your industry? Will training or exposure to new and different management areas give you fresh skills that might be transferable to a new area in the industry, should that become interesting to you? Will the demands of this new post create new or different stress on your personal life? How short-lived and manageable will those pressure points be? Do you have the support you need at home to make this move in a positive, upbeat, winning way?

Will you be a better employee, manager, contributor, leader, and human being for taking this post? Take the time to examine and visualize yourself in this new place. Be honest about the task at hand and the people you will be working with and reporting to. If you are excited by the challenge as well as the whole opportunity and see little downside risk on the other end, you might decide to give it your all and make a go of it. Try to recognize the idealistic and romantic tendencies you might have when considering something new and exciting, as you hold the realistic road map in your mind's eye, with your feet solidly planted on the ground.

ASSUME YOUR NEXT ROLE

Work, act, and think the way you would in your next job. If you want to be a manager, display the necessary attributes before the opportunity is even available. Become the "natural hire" for every rung up the ladder.

The way you conduct yourself on a daily basis speaks volumes compared with an hour's worth of interview when the job you want is open. You cannot sell yourself as an idea person if you haven't contributed effective ideas over the past 12 months. You cannot sell yourself as a leader if you have not spurred your team on to new ideas or led them through a recent change. In short, you cannot portray yourself as one type of employee if you have not displayed that proficiency in your daily work.

> *You cannot portray yourself as one type of employee if you have not displayed that proficiency in your daily work.*

Poise, language, leadership, and team play each count as much as an astute business mind does. A positive mental attitude and the ability to articulate a vision in a way that motivates others are important assets to any career and company. Inclusive behavior and respect for diverse ideas are two of the "soft" attributes that make great leaders. You must have consistent results in your bag as a given, for these are the measurable, tangible, hard-core metrics you can present about yourself. These softer attributes are more difficult to measure because they are the grains of enthusiasm, esprit de corps, creativity, and motivation that are sprinkled on the population that you affect. The best managers and most-often-tapped leaders possess both: the ability to execute plans with skill and efficiency and the personal power to positively and passionately move others.

If you are, or want to be, a manager with growth potential to executive level, then manage your work and affect your team with the same competencies that you admire in the company management force. Take advantage of any offered training within the company, or take initiative and expand your education with adult education courses. Be innovative in your ideas, motivating in your passion, positive in your attitude, and empathetic toward those around you. Be aware of what is critical to your company's success and to your manager's well-being. Do promote yourself to your manager and to your champion, through periodic meetings, written reports, and certainly at your annual reviews.

Be innovative in your ideas, motivating in your passion, positive in your attitude, and empathetic toward those around you.

QUESTIONS

- Are you aware of what you'd like your next move to be?

- Are you learning, from those in the position currently, what it takes to do the job with excellence?

- Do you exhibit skills on a daily basis that prove your ability to face the next challenge?

- Which skills have you identified in your company's leadership that you'd like to emulate? What is driving you to make a move now?

- How will a career shift affect your whole life and your future life plans?

- Do you have the personal support that will make your move less stressful?

- What are the opportunity risks? Money, time commitment, job duration, stress, politics, people?

- Who will you be reporting to and working beside? How do you feel about these people?

- Will this next job move you on your proposed course?

- Are you making the decision to take a new job based on ego because you were "chosen"?

- How much do you trust your management to take care of you after this job has been delivered?

- What is the downside to not accepting a position that you were asked to take but you don't want?

- Is staying in good graces and following someone else's plan for you worth taking a job that you are sure that you don't want?

- How long will you let yourself stay in a job that you love and have mastered?

- How long can you stay in one position before the company considers you a roadblock?

SUMMARY OF PART II: EXCEL, EXECUTE, ENJOY!

■ Value yourself if you intend to be valuable to an organization and industry. Begin by defining the personal core values that you live by and want to see reflected in your workplace. The more your values match the company's, the higher your chances for a smooth and fulfilling career.

■ Flourish and thrive in tough times or through change by embracing your values and consistently delivering excellent work. Take the high road by propelling action, shunning negative language, speculation and gossip.

■ Use the tough times as a learning proposition. See which leaders you admire most, who your friends are and gain a new understanding of why difficult business decisions have to be made sometimes.

■ Understand why a goal is a goal and how it affects the company and your unit so that you might deliver breakthrough work. Dispatch complete work, on time, every time. Ask for clarity rather than deliver work that is off the mark. Don't go down alone with a business problem because surprises will backfire on you. Spend time each day to review your work; be a thinker as well as a doer. Learn what is working well and where you can improve.

- Keep an eye on the cost side of your business plan. Reduce excessive spending, make your area as efficient as possible, ask your customers for a road map to success, cut redundancy to free up your time, admit mistakes openly, make suggestions for a better workplace, use your expense account wisely and celebrate success.

- Take charge of the perceptions about you in the workplace. Deliver solid work; monitor your conduct and language; act, work, and think in concert with the company values that you admire. Forge a trust with your management based on consistency, integrity and sound judgement. Choose to be a haven to your manager in difficult times; don't be an alarmist.

- Try very hard to empathize with your stressed manager or colleague. You might see that you are more crucial than you imagined to this person and place. If you expect certain (negative) behaviors from people who are famous for delivering them, then don't be surprised when they come through. Be the calm in a storm and don't take it personally.

- Be prepared in meetings so that your work is never in question. Avoid faking an answer and opt to admit when you don't know something.

- Always ask for feedback if you need information on your performance or about promotions lost. Learn, ask, absorb and do. Make your goals known to your manager and to human resources so that you are on the radar screen when opportunities arise.

- If you see something that you believe to be a wrong in the workplace, take action. You will learn much about the integrity of your company and its leaders and you will inform yourself about your own values. Staying silent could hurt your company, your objectives and yourself.

- Identify the companies that you want to work for by creating a competency list that matches your own values. Be aware of companies that offer stretch, training, succession planning and have solid reputations for leadership as well as growth.

- Realize that your questions are a clue to your thinking; use them as a competitive advantage. Take every opportunity to glean information that will help you to decide if you want to work at this organization and for the person you are meeting with. Leave compensation to a final meeting in the process. If the salary falls short, decide how important the difference is versus your opportunity for growth, learning and keeping you on your personal (whole life) goal path.

- Your manager is your most important contact and can help to make your career great or your life miserable. Pick with great care and learn what you can about style, background, motivation, and if he or she is champion potential for you. Identify the areas that you are in concert with and those in which you differ to create strategies to gain a thriving relationship in spite of any differences.

- Your annual review is important and will speak to people who don't know you personally. Take the time to be proactive for the meeting through preparation and anticipation. Do create the exhibits outlined in Chapter 19 as this will help you in your day-to-day fulfillment as well as readiness for the actual meeting.

- Understand what motivates you so that you will be aware of why you want your next post. Be honest with yourself regarding ego and how a move will impact your whole life, presently and for the future. Don't take a job that you don't want simply because you were "chosen." What is in it for you?

- Don't be in so much of a hurry that you move up before you master your current role. Sometimes it is very nice to relax in a place and enjoy the fruits of your labor in a position that you have conquered.

- The way that you handle yourself on a daily basis speaks volumes compared with an hour's worth of interview when the job you want is open.

III PLANNING FOR PASSION AND PROSPERITY

KINGMAKER

21 Branding Yourself: The Art of Free Agency

Free agency must be an actual goal in your career today. Economic conditions and technological advances intimidate the workforce as never before. Free agency in this context does not mean becoming a freelancer. It means that although you are loyal and valuable to the organization that you work for, you are also a "get" in your industry. Your goal is to be the one your company wants to keep and other companies want to steal away. You want to become the "wow" that everyone wants to hire. There is no better freedom earned than to know that you have career security based on your consistently excellent work, measurable results, passion, and integrity. Free agency does not mean that job-hopping becomes a goal, only that it is an option if you need or want it. Note that a résumé with too many changes begs questions. Nothing beats loving the place you work and being counted as an important, productive, and contributing member of the A-team.

> *Your goal is to be the one your company wants to keep and other companies want to steal away. You want to become the "wow" that everyone wants to hire.*

A Lesson in Free Agency

I became a free agent by accident. When Capitol Cities bought ABC in 1985 they also sold the television station I worked for at the time. My initial career plan, to stay with ABC for my working life, was derailed. Painful as it was, it proved fruitful because I moved fearlessly forward, met many bright folks, learned different strategies, and earned a healthy view of competition. I came to appreciate the importance of my own integrity to the company and marketplace, staying current with product knowledge, growing contacts, and always embracing change. I learned through understanding objectives, in a big-picture sense, I could grow my value to a company and an industry. I also greatly out-earned annual raises and believe I reached higher levels faster by changing company affiliations. ■

If you are strong, invested, productive, intelligent, ethical, energetic, and compassionate, you will earn your own free agency. The components of free agency include consistency, competitive product knowledge, and industry contacts. Becoming a free agent while productively employed is an ongoing consideration and it need not be difficult if you are already committed to the ideals of excellence, truth, anticipation and planning. The road map to your own free agency is:

All of the listed criteria are already part of your career competencies today.

- Consciously deliver quality work with dignified behavior on a consistent basis.
- Create your own board of directors.
- Choose to work for companies with respected leadership.
- Stay abreast of industry trends.
- Continue your on-going education.
- Grow contacts and relationships within your company and industry.

If this seems daunting to you because you are so busy right now you can't even think about these items, take minute to consider them. All of the listed criteria are already part of your career competencies today. The only suggested addition is that you become aware of them as a means to job security beyond your current place of employment. Realize that you don't have to want to leave your current company; rather, this is an insurance policy against a change you might not see coming. You don't have to do all of these things all of the time, either. For example, trends, education, and contacts aren't occurring all the time.

Consciously Deliver Quality Work with Dignified Behavior on a Consistent Basis

Be mindful of your actions and your motives in your business life. Build a name for yourself as a person who gets things done, understands and serves the customer, knows how to ethically exploit any situation to the good of the company, is a genuine team player, and stays true to his or her personal values. Become your customer's go-to person externally as well as internally, through anticipation and planning. Decide that respect trumps being liked, but understand that if you treat people with the respect that you want for yourself, you will have both. Act with dignity and you will be treated in a dignified manner. Be passionate and positive about your mission and you will ignite others and raise the level of your work environment. You get what you give in the long run, even if that means making difficult or painful decisions along the way.

> Leave on a high note and realize that you are smarter and richer for having been at this place, even if the circumstances were hellish at times. You will reap the benefits in your new workplace and in the gains derived for your whole life.

Be results-oriented through intelligence, strategy, will, and team play. Lead and act with compassion and wisdom. Some elements of compassion are generosity, ethics, concentration, patience, and effort. Which of these don't belong in business as much as any part of your life? Wisdom is in the culmination of the attributes of compassion, and in knowing what you don't know as much as what you do know.

If you change companies, leave on honorable terms in as much as you can control the situation. If you find yourself in an untenable situation, work to stay grounded so that any moves you make are measured and not based on emotion. Take the high road even if you'd love to scream at somebody or laugh in his or her face. Leave on a high note and realize that you are smarter and richer for having been at this place, even if the circumstances were hellish at times. You will reap the benefits in your new workplace and in the gains derived for your whole life.

COOL AS A CUCUMBER, STRONG AS STEEL

I've mentioned an acting lesson earlier in this book that is so fruitful as a tool for business that it bears repeating. I've used this exercise before making presentations and through tense times, such as leaving a job in difficult circumstances. It works. Sometimes when an actor has to become a character, he or she has difficulty conjuring up the needed emotions for the part. For example, the role might call for someone strong and the actor doesn't feel strong, or sexy, or angry . . . you get the picture. The trick is to call up people or things in the universe that have the characteristics you are looking to find within yourself. Decide on a person or item and list the characteristics that are relevant. Act your way into being that energetic presenter when you'd just as soon go home! I employed this acting technique when I was trying to leave a company through a very strained situation. I am a hot person and I needed to be very cool. I wanted to leave a certain company with severance, have the summer off, and land a management job in the market, all at the same time.

I realized that this was an incredibly tall order and I searched for people and things in the universe that are cool; I came up with the simple and common cucumber. A cucumber is thick-skinned and, coming from the ground, it is earthy. A cucumber is versatile because it can be eaten alone or in a salad. It is refreshing and cool. Every morning for two weeks I transformed myself in the shower. I practiced and meditated on being earthy, thick-skinned, refreshing, versatile, and cool. This helped me a great deal. I achieved all three of my objectives and becoming a cucumber was a great alternative to Murder One! ■

The way you leave a company is important because it can have future effects on your career and reputation. Realize that any move is about your future, not the past that brought you to it. You might need a reference for the next job, you don't want to be labeled a problem, and you could even end up working with some of the same people in another place. You will likely run into these players at industry functions, and who needs the tension? You will be remembered at a company as much for the way you leave as for the good works you contributed while you were there.

Realize that any move is about your future, not the past that brought you to it.

Keep your expectations in line regarding the reaction you will receive when you give notice. What will reasonably exasperate an employer? Is your departure going to ignite it?

- You're a "get" in the industry and perceived as a player in the company. Your leaving will be a loss and possibly an embarrassment.

- You've been with the company for less than a year and you've received excellent training and been part of a great environment. Your leaving could be taken personally, as an affront and an insult to the invested manager: "How could he leave this place after all we've invested in him?"

- You are going to a chief competitor and you have important company knowledge that could aid your new company. Even if you have acted with the highest integrity, there will be fear that you will divulge important information. (Note: If you move to a company that expects or invites you to give former company secrets, you might question their integrity. The ethical move is to keep secrets and not use them as leverage in your new place.)

If your ride has been bumpy, with many arguments, don't be surprised if your manager is relieved that you've decided to leave. If you have been regarded as a threat to the status quo and the management doesn't want change, they might not be sorry to see you go either.

If you are the subject of a headcount reduction, or even fired, you still have to be conscious of the way you depart an organization. You might jeopardize a financial exit package if you act up, so the loss would be all yours. Depending on the level of anger or mistrust on the part of your management, you could find your computer locked or your work purged. Things can get nasty. I've seen occasions where a year's worth of e-mail was pulled and examined in case the fired party chose to sue. You might be walked out by a security guard, paraded in front of yesterday's peers. If that is the company policy, it's not a big deal. If it is not regular policy and you are walked out, you'll look like a dead man walking.

> *Depending on the level of anger or mistrust on the part of your management, you could find your computer locked or your work purged. Things can get nasty.*

If you are fired outright and it is a complete surprise to you, think about it: Do you want to work for a company, or a person, who had not given you ongoing input that your job was in jeopardy? Are you being fired or demoted to make way for the new manager's "people"? Realize this is a no-win situation. You wouldn't have an easy time working for someone who doesn't want you there or would rather have someone else. On the other hand, can you say to yourself that you were an invested and contributing member of the organization? Do you know, in the pit of your stomach, that you weren't a great employee? Take responsibility and use the occasion for some key learning about yourself, then move forward with new knowledge that will not put you in the same place again.

To reiterate, keep your end goals in mind: You want to leave on the best possible terms and move on with your life. Stay focused on your goal and realize that your departure, on whatever terms, is about you and the next step in your life and career. The past is over and rehashing in anger won't change anything except what might be said about you in the future. If you have an opportunity at an exit package, muster all the patience and calm that you can so that you don't minimize or lose it. Just get through the drama and move on with your life.

CREATE YOUR OWN BOARD OF DIRECTORS

From time to time you will need people with whom you can brainstorm serious and important decisions. Create your own informal "board of directors" by including friends and colleagues that you trust and respect and whose opinions and outlook can aid you in coming to decisions that suit your short and long-term goals, personality, and character. Take input from this group, but have your own counsel be the deciding factor, because you have to live with your decisions. You know your true self better than anyone else ever can.

- How important is the decision you need to make in terms of your long-term career and life goals?
- Can you make the choice on your own or is it complex and you need some help with it?
- Who are the people you naturally go to when you need a sounding board or a fresh outlook?
- Does this problem require input from people outside of your normal circle?

As you mull over your decision, consider the parts of the problem you are least familiar with and see if you can include someone that has the experience with it that you lack. Are your new concerns about a job function, a bad boss, a company or career change, a geographical move, an open-ended post that could derail your long-term goal?

List the pros and cons. Examine the con portion and list the information required to make a rational decision against each item. Who among the people you know and respect has the experience or insight to aid you?

Think about the elements of the decision you need to make and list the pros and cons. Examine the con portion and list the information required to make a rational decision against each item. Who among the people you know and respect has the experience or insight to aid you? Can you count on these people to give you honest insights into your personality and style and how to become more compatible with a difficult boss? Will the people you choose be willing to play devil's advocate, even if you don't want to hear their contrary view? You must seek the opposing view so that you can consider the issue full circle and test your un-comfort zone enough to consider what that would feel like long term. Who can you role-play with so that you might uncover new questions and solutions and prepare yourself for a healthy discussion once your final answer is derived?

Pick people who have experience and wisdom on the subject you are pondering. Create your own board of directors by including experienced people who know you well. Have the courage to involve people who will be able to empathize with your situation while they offer a different view to help you make your decision.

The book *Decide & Conquer: Understanding and Improving How You Make Decisions* by Stephen P. Robbins, Ph.D., is a solid resource for deeper personal insights and the actual decision-making process.

CHOOSE TO WORK FOR COMPANIES WITH RESPECTED LEADERSHIP

Becoming a high-potential employee in a *Fortune* 500 company with highly regarded leadership and good "Street vitals" strengthens your résumé. Wall Street is attracted to businesses with solid earnings and a good price-to-earnings ratio that also grow strong management, with a healthy bench, through succession planning.

When a manager has an opportunity to hire someone, experience in a solid organization brings positive assumptions and associations to the candidate, even before there is a first meeting. It might be presumed that if you passed muster and were hired, and possibly promoted, at a company that they consider a role model or chief rival, you will have learned a great deal about discipline, process, accountability, and the industry. When your background includes a top company

When your background includes a top company known for stretch, creativity, and intelligence, you have scored points going into the interview.

known for stretch, creativity, and intelligence, you have scored points going into the interview.

Decide on the elements that you want to see in the company you work for and tailor your search to include these characteristics. You want to grow, so you want training, stretch, great leadership, a good manager to report to, and you want a champion. If you work for a company that invests in its people and creates and revises succession plans, you will be more likely to reach your goals within that company. Remember that the more the company's values and yours match, the more likely it is that you will have a successful and enjoyable track there.

Stay Abreast of Industry Trends, Ongoing Education, and Growing Contacts and Relationships Within Your Company and Industry

If you are working for a company that believes in developing its A players, take advantage of every possible training perk. Ask about extra training in your job interviews and volunteer for the course work whenever it is made available. Anything that you can learn, that is pertinent to your industry and to your growth, *and* that is paid for by someone else is an absolute no-brainer. It is a compliment to be included in training because it is expensive and your selection means that you, your service and your future potential for the company are valued.

I worked at a place that had an awesome and deep regard for training. We worked with a consultant to customize sales and marketing courses for our company-wide sales force. The training was held off-site and was one to three days in duration, once or twice a year, for two years. All sales employees were required to go and we were the only company among our major competitors who included this heavy training in the workload. I was amazed on two counts. First, many employees thought that the training was a real burden. The people in this company worked hard as a given and being taken away from their ongoing work felt like more work to some. Some people, who were very good at what they did and did not aspire beyond their level, felt the course work was actually needless. The second count was that our competition tried to use their lack of training as a perk to steal our (trained) people away!

> *Our competition tried use their lack of training as a perk to steal our (trained) people away! If you are with a company that "burdens" you with extra learning, try hard to see the merits.*

If you are with a company that "burdens" you with extra learning, try hard to see the merits. You get a breath of fresh air outside of your normal routine. You get to start and grow relationships with people in your company from different areas of the country or division. You have the opportunity to learn and grow and gain a real competitive advantage and a stronger résumé than your probable competition. You might get a fresh perspective on the repetitive, "same old," of your daily work.

You can also keep abreast of industry changes by speaking with the leaders of your company to see what is new and exciting to them. Perhaps you could incorporate a "specialist" in your regular meetings who will report on fresh news of interest in your industry, including your competition and the businesses that are major revenue contributors to your company and to your rivals.

Another popular training tactic is to bring company leaders or outside professionals to your workforce to speak about an area of your industry, new research, or trends that might affect your business. This broadens scope and creates beyond-the-norm thinking. I once created a speaker's series and it was very well received, even among the people that felt burdened by the longer form training. The meetings were held monthly on Friday mornings and included topics that the workforce wanted covered.

Occasional adult education courses can broaden your horizons and keep you up to date in a fast-changing world. New knowledge will serve to refresh your passions and make you the "get." Although these courses might be at your own expense, consider that your career potential is worth the investment.

Read trade journals and network within your industry by joining associations and mentor groups. Some associations will have different task forces, which you can join or at least learn about. This is another opportunity to meet people within your industry that could grow into future liaisons. This can sound like a lot on top of your heavy workload, but networking functions and classes are not necessarily constant, and they can be an ongoing source of refreshment and growth for you.

Work with passion, empathy, and dignity and treat all those who surround you with regard. Raise the bar in the workplace; make a difference through your consistent attitude and results. After all is said and done, the way you spend each day matters to your whole life and to your free agency.

QUESTIONS

- Are you a "get" in your industry?

- Will you keep expectations in mind when you give notice to your current company?

- Will you do whatever is possible to leave your company on good terms, no matter the situation?

- Who can you name to your own personal board of directors?

- What are the specific elements that you need to consider to make a grounded decision?

- How are the leaders of your company regarded in your industry?

- Do you enjoy extra training? Can you respect its merits enough to embrace it?

- If you find extra training burdensome, what can you do to change your outlook and enjoy new learning? What are the personal benefits from this training?

- Do you take the time to read trade publications? Perhaps devote one lunch hour a week to reading them?

- Are you well known and highly regarded within your industry?

- Can you create a plan that includes a class or two and some networking opportunities throughout the year that will keep you updated, refreshed, and well known?

- What steps will you take to enhance your career and your sense of value and security?

22 ACHIEVING FULFILLMENT THROUGH GREAT WORK

Y ou will thrive more fluently if you are able to engage in work that is fulfilling to your sense of purpose at a company that has values in concert with your own. It is worth your effort to make this compatibility one of your career goals so that you can develop most fully and enjoy your working experience most effortlessly.

We read a lot about people pursuing fulfillment on the job, but most advice is to follow your dreams and make it happen, posthaste. "Prepare, drop everything and go to your dream" seems to be the rallying cry. There is good news and bad news as it relates to this guidance.

> The people, places, and activities you are surrounded by impact your energy and your values. Because you don't always get to pick those elements, the way that you approach your situations will make all the difference.

The good news is that following your passions and keeping your dreams alive are worthy goals for a fulfilled and purposeful life. The bad news is that although it might be good and healthy to pursue your happiness by changing your career and your life, it is not always prudent or available if the time for you to make a whole shift isn't right. As you move through your career you will have ups and downs. This is normal and will facilitate growth of the career and personal kind. As you proceed, hold on to your passions by incorporating them into your daily work as much as you can or keeping them in sight until the day you can get to them.

It might not be available or right if you aren't prepared, or clear on what you want to do next. It might not be an option if you are the chief wage earner and your family cannot afford a large cut in salary right now. It might not be a good idea if you are in a bad mental or emotional space and you aren't able to muster the energy and creativity to make the big move. Finally, it might not be quite the right time if you are making great money but have not yet met the financial base goal that you need to securely make such a move.

Although it is purposeful to move toward your dream, doing it at the right time, when you are in the right mental and financial state will go a long way toward making your dreams come true. This is not to advocate forgetting your dreams; rather, keep your dreams and work toward them so that you can move to them when the time is right for you in most every area. Try to let your dream be your overriding goal as you make each day as good as it can possibly be.

Fulfillment is personal and not to be confused with productivity or activity. Being busy is not the same as feeling that you are a contributing member of society or that you are learning and growing or helping someone to do the same. For some, fulfillment means being a full person whose values guide their actions. The people, places, and activities you are surrounded by impact your energy and your values. Because you don't always get to pick those elements, the way that you approach your situations will make all the difference.

> *How do you get unstuck enough to change your world view without having to change your whole world?*

The people and activities that you can choose to immerse your world in have the power to constantly refresh your energy and value system. The infusion of fresh energy and outlook can go a long way toward making a bad day good, so do what you can to make this a priority in and outside of your working lives.

What if you are on the way to being miserable and can't make a move yet? How do you get unstuck enough to change your world view without having to change your whole world? How about doing everything possible to make your current work and workplace more enjoyable and fulfilling? Reignite the elements of fulfillment that you yearn for within the work and company that you have now, while you continue to work toward your bigger dream.

First gauge your current level of fulfillment or unfulfillment. Break it down as far as possible by examining the people, the job, and the agony to revenue ratio (job/pay) and see if you can find the root of your malaise. Use the checklist in Table 22-1 on the following page as the beginning of your examination and first step in becoming free of your contrary groove. This is not to dwell on negative aspects; it is to uncover the issues and how they make you feel so that you can create a plan to do something about it now.

When you are able to zero in on the root of your dilemma you will be better prepared to create a plan to do something about it. Many of these listed issues have been covered in previous sections of this book. Revisit those earlier chapters and get involved with the questions to find your own answers. You might find one or two areas that can make an immediate difference in your happiness and fulfillment quotient. You might begin to pursue your creative tendencies in the workplace through negotiation with your noncreative boss, or find a way to work with a manager who has given you difficulty in the past. Find the courage to go to human resources or to your management with the perceived problem and your proposed solutions. Discover the troubling issue and take action to create your personal solution to lessen the negativity.

> *If you reach a point where the internal political situations are becoming toxic to your spirit or unmanageable within your value system, you must be able to sublimate their importance, affect positive change, find other means for an influx of positive energy, or give yourself the time to plan your departure.*

If you reach a point where the internal political situations are becoming toxic to your spirit or unmanageable within your value system, you must be able to sublimate their importance, affect positive change, find other means for an influx of positive energy, or give yourself the time to plan your departure. Are you always striving to "make a difference" in the things you do? Maybe now is the time to turn this cliché onto yourself.

TABLE 22-1 Satisfaction Checklist

ISSUE	HOW IT MAKES ME FEEL			
	Okay	Unsure	Unsafe	Unfulfilled
Management Changes				
Bad Boss				
Stagnant Leadership				
Stifled Creativity				
24/7 Mental Attention to Work				
Lack of Attribution				
Lack of Champion				
Feelings of Exclusion				
Uncomfortable as Politician				
Politics Too Thick and Unnerving				
Cronyism				
Lack of Respect From Peers and/or Management				
Headcount Reduction Mentality				
Tough Job Market				
Ageism, Sexism, Racism				
Lack of Personal Savings				
Debt				
Loss of Interest				
Not My Passion				
Job-Related Anxiety, Depression				

Discover the ways to make a difference in your sense of peace and happiness so that you can be free to flourish. One way to begin to bring your job enjoyment goals to life is to get out of your own head. Infuse a sense of spirituality into your workday and see if this can help to brighten it.

Start with the environment in your workplace. If you are fortunate to be in surroundings where people are valued and treated in a respectful way, all the better. Whether you are in a positive workplace or not, realize that your presence makes a difference to the atmosphere and to actual goal execution. You are able to tuck this essence into your daily work.

Your work matters and it's important that you treat your career as if it is noble, as if it is bigger than you are. Great work is not only about you, but also about what it can do for the greater good. Your work impacts your colleagues, the company, the town you live in, the state it is a part of, the country it serves, and the global audience that will use your product or service. Yes, you will benefit directly from the effort, but the action has a larger scope than serving just your personal benefit. Seeing this larger picture might give your efforts a deeper, more meaningful resonance.

Bringing a spiritual aspect to the job doesn't mean being soft on hard work and it doesn't mean that you're suddenly religious if you're not. It means finding a way to make the work bigger than what goes on in your head, and it might help you to pay less attention to the negative people or political aspects when they occur. It means finding joy, exuberance, and fulfillment in your great effort and the effects of that effort on the world, no matter how big or small, or what it is that you do for a living. Adding a spiritual sense to your daily work could be as simple as acknowledging that you are a part of a whole and that you matter to the spirit, productivity, creativity, and morality of that whole. It means applying your mental and emotional energies to the atmosphere, but especially to the work. The work itself reaches a higher manifestation as you approach it with dignity, probity, ethics, and respect. Nothing feels greater than to work flat-out with high energy, feeling strong, and on a mission that you believe in, while moving others to positive action along with you. Action and respect for the purpose of the work

> *Acknowledge that you are part of a whole and that you matter to the spirit, productivity, creativity and morality of that whole. The work itself reaches a higher manifestation as you approach it with dignity, probity, ethics and respect.*

has the power to change the feel, the pace, and the position of a workplace.

When you have a rough moment, little aids in your workspace such as the placement of art, flowers, family pictures, a fishing pole, or some other personal talisman can help you through. Taking a walk around the block or finding a quiet place nearby for some deep breathing can also offer a way to cope and bring you back to the spirit of great work. This surely beats punching a wall, crying in public, or screaming your head off . . . and I've seen all three.

As early as 1982 I found watching the skaters at Rockefeller Center or sitting in the back of a dark and quiet St. Patrick's Cathedral to be very soothing and stabilizing for me. After a few minutes I could return to the workplace with a freshly centered approach. I knew the work was more important than the games that people played and I applied myself to it with great spirit. I made my work and its purpose more important than the toxic incivility that was sometimes present. In hindsight I see that I might even apply myself more ardently in rough times than in calm times. It's as if the work can heal and refocus the energy to something higher and much more meaningful than the egotistical maniac who just walked over you or a colleague. The bad guy doesn't have to matter so much if you take away the power of the ridiculous behavior by minimizing its effect on your mind and your soul.

It's as if the work can heal and refocus the energy to something higher and much more meaningful than the egotistical maniac who just walked over you or a colleague.

We do have choices in how we spend parts of our day and whom we spend it with. We have choice in the type of person we want to grow into and it is our own will and character that help us define the road to it. Breaking free from your stranglehold might take all of your ability and determination and it will require your tenacity and belief in your worthiness of a better life.

Resources include your own board of directors, HR departments, credit consolidators, church leaders, therapists, books, the Internet, and so on. You can find the roads to your answers if you want to. Gather support in the form of people you trust and people who love you and make your plan for a better life. Give yourself patience and time to do your best to change a bad situation and be kind to yourself. Just knowing you have a long-term passion plan will help keep you grounded and calm as you keep your eyes on the fulfillment prize.

QUESTIONS

- Do you find your work fulfilling or purposeful?

- If not, what is blocking this aspect?

- If you want to make a career change can you do it now?

- If no, what can you do to make your current place purposeful and fulfilling?

- Can you pinpoint the root cause of your discontent?

- Are you willing to put your energy into making a difference for yourself?

- What is the highest purpose of your work to the community?

- Which personal articles can you put in your workspace to calm you down when you need it?

- Can you identify surroundings in your area that bring you calm if you need a quick escape?

- Do you fill your nonworking hours with people and activities that replenish your spirit?

- What sort of plan can you put together that will put you on the road to your dream and passion?

23 LETTING GO AND HAVING A LIFE

Keeping your life balanced while pursuing a career isn't always easy, but making balance a priority in your life is a healthy way to go. Some people are decidedly one-tracked or passion-skewed, and I think I was one of those. Are you? At very pressurized times, I didn't know how to give my all to work and have enough energy or time left over to nourish the other facets of my life. It takes a clear mind to realize that giving your all doesn't mean giving everything. In time you will begin to desire and seek better parity for parts of life that might have been ignored. Priorities and outlook change as situations change and as you grow.

It takes a clear mind to realize that giving your all doesn't mean giving everything.

Examine your investment level in your current job and decide if you are at about the right pace or if you're a bit over the top. What is driving your drive? Is it passion? Is it that you love your work and it makes you happy? Is it fear that you aren't doing enough and you're worried about losing your job? Could you have a time or priority management problem that needs to be improved? Are you using your work to escape from other parts of your life that you don't want to be involved with? Do you work in a culture that rewards people who relentlessly give to the office without time for personal recharge? Is your drive monetary? Is your job constantly demanding, or are you in a period where extra time is needed, expected, and warranted? For example, if you are an accountant, you expect to work night and day from January to April 15.

You have to be willing to unplug, or at least review your working habits so that you give yourself the time and the space to have a full life and recharge. If fear is driving you, perhaps you aren't receiving enough positive feedback about your work and your company's commitment to you. Ask for it. Let your manager know that you are feeling pressed, you take pleasure in your work, but that the load might be unhealthy to your overall job contribution and other aspects of your life. Ask for the commitment; ask for feedback. Listen to the good reviews that you get and let them lead you to relax a bit. Working in frenzy without fresh input from people or leisure activities that you enjoy isn't healthy, and you probably aren't working at your best level, even if you're working all the time.

If you need to work weekends because that's the only time you can catch up on e-mail or write the necessary memo or paper, do it. However, do it as a form of confident expectation of the hour when you can relax. Set a time limit that doesn't interfere with personal activities. If that means writing at 5 A.M. so that you can make your 7:30 tee time, do it. If you want to spend time with your family or friends, try to schedule the hours you need to work around the activity, rather than the other way around.

> *If you need to work weekends, set a time limit that doesn't interfere with personal activities. If that means writing at 5 A.M. so that you can make your 7:30 tee time, do it. If you want to spend time with your family or friends, try to schedule the hours you need to work around the activity, rather than the other way around.*

Take your vacations and if you can help yourself, don't call in to the office. One of the competencies of great managers is that their unit is so well prepared it can function without them. The same should be true at any job level. You do a great job and you have teammates that you can trust to cover for you while you are out. You have a committed manager who won't let your work fall through the cracks and you don't leave before you write a document that will fill the expectations for your coverage and all important contact numbers. You can leave a phone number where you can be reached in case of an emergency, which should ease your mind about leaving for a short time.

Do a great job, but live a great life, too.

I attended a writer's workshop where Jan Phillips, author of the award-winning *Marry Your Muse*, spiritual teacher, and workshop director, was a speaker. Jan taught us how to reach sacred spirituality through honorable work.[1] She moved me as she articulated thoughts on how to achieve a full and balanced life dedicated to the honor of your life and your God. Among many other life-pertinent lessons, Jan Phillips teaches that fullness and gratification come from at least four areas in a full life. These areas are the mental, emotional, spiritual, and physical. Keeping a balance across these four focus points is not always easy and we are usually not conscious of them as separate entities because one can have an impact on another, and we're often too busy to notice anyway. I always thought balance meant having quality time with family and friends outside of my business to provide me with perspective on the arts or current events, or anything outside of the television milieu. It took many years for me to understand that balance is truer and fuller when the mental, emotional, spiritual, and physical aspects of a full life are considered.

> *Fullness and gratification come from at least four areas in a full life. These areas are the mental, emotional, spiritual, and physical.*

One of Jan's exercises had us draw a circle and break it into the four areas. We were given time to think about our interests and activities and the people who fill our lives. The next step was to place each item or person in the appropriate segment of the circle. What I found was that a whole area was practically empty, another was overflowing, and several items spanned multiple sections. Just through this quick exercise I was able to see where I was out of kilter, and it led me to think about activities, interests, and people that could help me balance my circle.

---

1. Jan Phillips Seminar: Creativity as Sacred Act. See *www.janphillips.com*.

Another way to help you to discover your passions and identify activities that can fill your fulfillment wheel is to think about how you see yourself. What is your identity? Who are you at your core? Who are you besides the title that you carry for 40 to 60 hours a week or more? Who are you beyond your paycheck and your business suit?

Keeping a fresh eye on all of what makes you you will help in your contentment pursuit. By any measure you are someone's child, sibling, friend, and employee; perhaps you are a parent and a spouse as well. You have interests and hobbies that are part of your sensuality and feed your mental, emotional, and spiritual spirits: cooking, writing, photography, knitting, art, yoga and meditation, volunteerism, music, or dance. You have physical interests that keep you strong mentally and emotionally: You run, work out, sail, golf, or take long walks . . . you move. These activities fill the four sectors and help give you a sense of gratification as they fill you up and contribute to a balanced life. You are each of these roles and interests.

You are more than your job, although your job can certainly partly fill these sectors. Mental exercise is a daily given. You feel emotion when you invest yourself in winning, on the occasion that you don't, and in doing a job well. Your adrenaline is sure to be running high when you are presenting, negotiating, or solving a conflict. Your spiritual sense is touched in the way you make your work bigger than you are and in the way you interact with those around you. Doesn't it feel rewarding to compliment someone's good work, help someone out of a jam, or thank somebody who helped you out of a tough predicament? Kind actions cost you nothing and the benefits come full circle.

> *You are more than your job, although your job can certainly partly fill these sectors.*

How can you incorporate and balance these four aspects into your busy life? I asked several friends and former associates how they were able to let go and have a life outside of work. Here are some of their answers:

- Literally stop and smell the roses.
- Take the time to consciously do at least one nice thing for another person each day, be it a stranger or a friend.

- Schedule exercise into your calendar and treat it as another appointment.
- Read books and listen to books on tape in the car or at the gym.
- Involve your family in community industry events when possible.
- Schedule your children's sporting and school events and go to them.
- Have a "date night" with your spouse (or love interest, or best friend) so that you stay connected.
- Practice mediation and yoga daily.
- Gather with good friends.
- Chardonnay.
- Golf.
- Rest at least one day a week and use the time for pure relaxation and a little reflection.
- Take every vacation day that you are allotted. Call in only when absolutely necessary (e.g., for an important meeting or to calm your obsessive head).
- Turn e-mail and your Blackberry off by a certain time each day.
- Get involved in community and church activities with your family.
- Volunteer two hours a week as a mentor (or at a children's hospital).
- Get seven to eight hours of sleep each night.
- Stress vegetables and protein, over sugar, in your diet.
- Take long hot baths, and get a regularly scheduled massage.
- Go fishing.

Take the time to draw a circle and fill in the four spaces for mental, emotional, spiritual, and physical. Sort the people and activities that are a part of your life into the appropriate sections; some might overlap. See how balanced you are, or are not, and give this some serious thought. What are the interests that you'd like to bring back or add to your life to make you a more well-rounded, fuller human being? Think about all the things you love and all the aspects of your life that can contribute to a more balanced you.

Take some action to find the time to stop. Work to feed all of your senses for a fuller you.

QUESTIONS

- Who are you besides the worker?

- What is your own private identity?

- What are your outside-work interests and how often do you partake in them?

- How do you fill the four sectors of fulfillment (mental, emotional, spiritual, physical)?

- Which segment is overloaded? Are any empty?

- Which rituals can you add to your daily calendar to ensure that you are more than your work?

- How does balance make you a happier and more centered human, family member, and worker?

- Do you take your vacations?

- What do you have to let go of to make room for these healthy additions to your life?

- Are you worth the commitment?

24 THE FREEDOM PLAN

Corporate life allows for great savings and investment opportunities. You work hard and hopefully are, or will be, in a position to earn a very good income. This chapter is devoted to encouraging you to take care of your money from the very beginning of your career. In doing so, you will have freedom of choice, more freedom from fear, and freedom to make your own decisions. You will be more attractive as an employee when you carry an air of confidence and independence because you are not motivated solely by money, but by productivity, results, and the enjoyment of learning, growing, and changing. You will have great personal joy in knowing that you are where you are because you want to be, rather than because you have to be.

> *Take care of your money from the very beginning of your career. In doing so, you will have freedom of choice, more freedom from fear, and freedom to make your own decisions. You will have great joy in knowing that you are where you are because you want to be, rather than because you have to be.*

I was 26 years old and had just been transferred to Chicago from my hometown of Detroit. I bought my first condo there. This was quite a time marking as it moved me into adulthood with debt and a tax write-off. I was quite excited by my cool space on Chestnut Street, nine blocks from the office and at the base of Rush Street. I came back to work after the closing and my boss came into my office. He asked me how the deal went and I said "Fine, no hitch," as I thought what a nice guy he was. He told me he was really happy I bought a place and then he asked me if I knew why. I told him I had no idea why he'd be so pleased, but it was very nice. At this, he held out his hand, palm side up, and put it in front of my face. He said, "You see this?" as he pointed to his palm. "I have you right here." I looked him in the eye, with all 26 years of haughty wisdom that I had, and said, "You never have me right here. If this doesn't work, I'll sell the condo or get another job." That was a good lesson to learn early: Never be stuck anywhere because of money.

> Never be stuck anywhere because of money.

I started to earnestly plan for the day I might want to leave 17 years before I said goodbye. When I began to see that dysfunction is often the rule rather than the exception, and that politics could be thick and uncomfortable, I knew that I wouldn't be willing or able to adapt beyond a certain point. I knew I'd want to be ready when the time came and I began to develop my freedom plan. This became part of my psyche and natural practice.

A Good Life

For the record, I am a first-generation American who grew up on the south side of Detroit, Michigan. We weren't rich, but I didn't know that as a kid because we always had lots of wonderful food, pretty clothes, great and fun vacations, and bountiful parties. We summered in Canada and sometimes Malta and wintered at Belle Isle, ice skating the afternoon away with a hot chocolate reward. My parents sent my siblings and me to Catholic school, an expense they deemed worthy for our education and value system. Some of the money mantras in our family were, "It's not how much you make, it's how much you save. Save for a rainy day. Don't worry about the Jones's." These ideas were drummed in early and often, but what I learned was that you could have a great life and still save for that rainy day, no matter your income or job title. ■

Money is a necessary ingredient for a freer life. A long-term financial plan allows for a good life while you plan for the time when you might need capital for a break, career change, early retirement, or perhaps to carry you over in a bad job or stock market. According to recent employment data, a person who earns less than $100,000 per year can assume it will take six months to find a new job. A person who earns more than $100,000 per year will need to budget for eight months. Wouldn't you like to be able to outlast the very worst job market and not have to start over at the very beginning?

There are many books, Web sites, cable shows, and broadcast programs to help you become more comfortable with financial planning. Certainly, this chapter is only a start, and I am not a financial guru. The following 10 considerations are an elementary discussion to explore your views on money, savings and investments, and your own attachment to material items or habits that might hamper your end goal. The road to financial freedom might seem daunting and undoable to some of you; please don't let that be enough to deter you from trying. Equal parts of patience, willingness, discipline, common sense, and determination are required to pay yourself the huge reward of peace of mind that comes with a freedom plan.

Consider these discussion points as a starter kit for your personal freedom plan.

1. What is your relationship with money?
2. Visualize your long-term goals: Retire early? Switch careers? Financial independence in your older years?
3. Freedom versus bondage. Freedom versus material goods. Create a value threshold.
4. Think like a corporation and protect your profit margin: your savings and investments.
5. Don't be afraid to bust conventional thinking.
6. How much money do you really need? How much is enough? Is enough enough?
7. Look good, take great vacations, and don't feel deprived.
8. Don't worry about what friends or family members say or think about your choices.

9. Be an active investor. Educate yourself and give time to your financial freedom plan.

10. Look into resources.

1. WHAT IS YOUR RELATIONSHIP WITH MONEY?

A relationship with money? Yes, we all have one, and it begins when we are children. It depends on how we react, as adults, to the early lessons learned. If you grew up in a household where money was no object, spending was free and lavish, and talk of savings was nonexistent, you will have one outlook. If your household was one where money was a bit tight, you might have felt it, and you might have disliked it. If you grew up in a home where money was discussed and the value of a dollar was a lesson that your parents impressed on you, you are more likely to be a saver now. There are households that surely had both: lots of money and lessons on its value.

What were your early lessons and how are you reacting to them in your adult life? Are money and the niceties that it affords part of your identity? Do you have the outlook that money will never be a problem, so you spend it freely? Are you a person who never had money and figure you never will, so you spend it freely? Do you have fears related to lack of money that find you a bit frugal? Do you view money as freedom? Is luxury spending something you do to reinforce a perception you have about yourself or the picture of the life that you want for yourself? What is your relationship with money and why do you think you have the disposition that you hold?

When you are able to understand your connection to money you will be better able to design your long-term plan. You might have to make some adjustments to your long-standing view and value system toward money to have a successful freedom plan. If you decide to take care of tomorrow while you are in your highest potential earnings years, you need to start as soon as possible.

The following questions are a brainstorming exercise toward a better understanding of your relationship with money:

- The lessons my parents taught by example were:
  (*fill in the blank*)
- I can't worry about tomorrow; it will take care of itself.
  true false
- I don't make enough money to start this plan yet.
  true false
- I can make little starts beginning today.
  true false
- I like nice things and what they say about me to others.
  true false
- I care about the impression other people have of me.
  none moderate extreme
- My friends have more money than I do and I want to keep up with them.
  true false
- Somebody will come into my life to take care of the financial aspects of our life.
  true false
- Credit cards are a financial aid.
  true false
- I work hard so why should I deny myself anything?
  true false
- I like nice things but they don't rule my decisions.
  true false
- I have a dream for a second career and I want to be able to afford it when the time comes.
  true false
- I'm not feeling very secure in this job market.
  true false
- I can see the day that I might top out in my field, or choose another one.
  true false
- I want to be ready for any eventuality.
  true false

■ I see that a freedom plan would be the best gift I could ever work toward.

true false

2. VISUALIZE YOUR LONG-TERM GOALS: WORK INTO YOUR 70S? RETIRE EARLY? SWITCH CAREERS? FINANCIAL INDEPENDENCE IN YOUR OLDER YEARS? SECURITY IN A BAD JOB OR STOCK MARKET?

This is where your self-knowledge comes in again. If you are 25 you might not even think about being 45, but it comes in a flash. Life brings surprises, challenges, and disappointments, and we cannot know the future. You don't have to have the answers now, but wouldn't it be great to be prepared for any eventuality? If you save for early retirement and decide, instead, to work into your old age, what is the harm in having a large net worth?

You can love your work and still see the peak of a chance that you might want to leave it relatively early in your life. Where do see yourself topping out in your field? What is the realistic outlook for your long-term career? Do you have a passion or dream that you'd like to turn into your life's work one day? Change points in your life can happen whether you choose the timing or it is forced upon you. How financially prepared will you be for either possibility? These questions beg consideration and the answers will help you decide when to begin your financial freedom planning.

3. FREEDOM VERSUS BONDAGE, FREEDOM VERSUS MATERIAL GOODS: CREATE A VALUE THRESHOLD.

Money gives you the opportunity to make choices freely. I cannot stress enough that in my own life and experience, having a solid financial cushion relieved a lot of anxiety when I was facing difficult choices or living in excruciating business circumstances. Just knowing I *could* move on helped me to stay sometimes, and it certainly fueled my courage when I decided to leave. I was able to make grounded decisions based on quality of life and work issues, free from any panic about where my next meal would come from.

We all like nice things and we work hard, so why shouldn't we have them? Examine your attachment to material items so that you will know how much money you really need to enjoy your life and feel good about yourself. You also should consider the concealed costs that come with some of the purchases you make. Examining your value thresholds will help you determine the time it will take for you to build a solid freedom plan.

Just knowing I could move on helped me to stay sometimes, and it certainly fueled my courage when I decided to leave.

Do you need to wear couture suits and shoes? Do you have to buy six new outfits a season, or can you spruce up an existing quality wardrobe with a few great items and some stunning, trendy accessories? Might you find it exciting to find fabulous items off-retail? Is spending $60,000 on a car a choice you'd make? Do you consider the higher insurance and maintenance costs that come with it? Do you have the same or a different value threshold toward other items such as good jewelry, art, and furniture? Must you stay in only the best hotels, or can you be happy in a moderate one? Can you switch off from time to time so that you can take more trips? Do you have to have the best house in the best neighborhood, which comes with the highest taxes, insurance, and maintenance fees? Can you find "home" in a more modest house in the same or the next-best neighborhood? Would you consider pioneering in what might be the next "hot" area and buy the best house there for the promise of higher equity growth potential?

Material items can bring us a feeling of accomplishment and enjoyment and they can show the world how well we're doing financially, at least on the surface. You need to know for yourself how material items stack up against your desire to have the freedom to make your own calls in life, or to take care of yourself and your family in tough times, if you have to. You can always have nice things; do you have to have all of the best things all of the time? Do you choose to spend your hard-earned money on material items that depreciate in value or accumulate assets that will grow in worth and help fulfill your current and long-term goals?

4. THINK LIKE A CORPORATION AND PROTECT YOUR PROFIT MARGIN: YOUR SAVINGS AND INVESTMENTS.

You will be ahead of the game if you apply the same disciplines and principles of financial management at home as you do in your workplace. Your costs are expenses and your income is your revenue. The amount of money that you have left is your own profit margin, your nest egg, or accrued wealth, Your profit builds your freedom plan. One goal is to have a designated amount targeted every year and trim expenses when necessary to meet it.

To fulfill your financial freedom plan, savings must become one of your regular expenses. You will become more aware of your savings pace when you actually count it as a part of your budget, beside housing, health, education, food, and taxes and above clothing, travel, and luxury items. Your goals will be reached more quickly and with less pain, as your savings become automatic. You will adapt to your new cash flow, spend within your designated means, and enjoy the comfort of knowing you are in a positively productive growth mode that will serve you very well, now and into the future.

The amount you can realistically save depends on the expenses you deem absolutely necessary. My rule of thumb was to save 20 percent of my gross income *on top* of my savings and investment plan.

What is your emotional attachment to the purchase you are considering versus your emotional attachment to never being stuck anywhere because of money?

When you consider a major purchase, conduct an assessment to determine if this new item is an asset accumulator or income drainer. Just as in business, you need to designate every capital expense as either a source of revenue or an expense.

- What are the hidden costs involved in owning a second home? Taxes, insurance, utilities, communications, landscaping, furniture, and maintenance are some. Will you need to buy another computer? Perhaps another car and more insurance? Will this investment grow your equity enough to recoup all of your ancillary cash outlay at the very least? Could you move it quickly if you are forced, or want to sell? How regularly will you use it?

- Should you upgrade your address and increase your monthly mortgage payments, insurance, and taxes? Will you become house poor? Will the increase in monthly costs to live in a better school system offset the expense for private school in your current area? Will you be able to realize substantial and rapid equity growth as much as an enjoyable growth in lifestyle?

- If you buy that boat, what are the hidden costs? Consider docking, gas, insurance, maintenance, dry-docking, and accessories.

- Will the luxury purchase of that boat, RV, or second home derail your saving and investment plan, or can you do both? Always consider what the odds are that you can you recoup your investment, and preferably realize a profit.

- What is your emotional attachment to the purchase you are considering versus your emotional attachment to never being stuck anywhere because of money?

5. DON'T BE AFTRAID TO BUST CONVENTIONAL THINKING.

Buster 1

It is very sensible to maximize your participation in all company-sponsored savings and investment plans. In many cases the company will match a certain percentage and you will also be able to save pretax dollars. The buster is that you must put this money away and not consider it usable toward the early part of your freedom plan. This is what I called "59½ -year-old money." You can access this money earlier if you need it, but penalties and taxes will apply. If you want to retire early or change careers, you need the capital to generate enough income to keep you happy from the time you make your change until you are 59½ years old. Your savings plan needs to include monies in addition to your 401(k).

Buster 2

Housing costs should not exceed 25 percent of your gross income. Why not make it 25 percent of your net income? You have to consider cash flow as it relates to your net, so why wouldn't you keep your (probably) largest monthly payment in line so that you can escape being house poor. One method that might help you get started is to estimate your annual tax write-off from the mortgage and plan your tax deductions to get a refund. Go for the stretch in your first year and bank the refund to supplement your mortgage payments for the ongoing years, so that your cash flow for mortgage payments does not exceed 25 percent of your net income.

6. How much money do you really need? How much is enough? Is enough enough?

You will need to do your homework, reach out to some resources, and continue your soul searching to get to these answers. The first order of business is to construct a budget if you don't already have one. Enter every possible expense that you can think of. Don't forget items such as vacations, dining out, charities, gifts, insurance, car maintenance or transportation, extra medical expenses, magazines and newspapers, sports, hobbies, and classes. Even enter items such as manicures, facials, or massages if you do this regularly.

Get a fix on what you spend each year and examine what is necessary, what could be cut down, and what could be cut out. A good, informative exercise is to create a spending diary. Write in every dollar you spend for a month and see what surprises you find. I created a diary after a panic attack, just before I was about to give my final notice. I was afraid that I didn't have enough money and would have to eat tomato sandwiches for the rest of my life. This fear ran through me even

> *Get a fix on what you spend each year and examine what is necessary, what could be cut down, and what could be cut out.*

though I had checked and rechecked my budget and financial plans many times. My surprise came with the amount of money I was spending on cabs and dry cleaning, both areas that could and did decline in my new life, but certainly not a block point to my plan. You will quickly see which drains your monies are going down and take steps to plug them.

Estimate your income and how it will grow between now and the time you will likely make your move. Decide whether to keep your savings percentage the same or increase it as your income grows. You will have more disposable income as your earnings rise, even if you keep the percentage the same, (i.e., 20 percent of $150,000 is higher than 20 percent of $50,000). You might see that you could easily afford to give yourself a raise! Another way to grow your savings is to invest most of any bonuses or incentive payouts after you buy a nice gift for yourself.

You can get a handle on your plan by building an income grid based on your age. Estimate your pension, 401(k), and Social Security income for the period of your life starting from that 59½-year benchmark. This will supplement the income you will derive from the base capital that you are building now. You need to estimate how many years' worth of budget you'll need to have to leave your job early. For example, if you want to leave at age 45, you will need 14½ years' worth of savings and investment income to live a comfortable life, assuming you don't have income from a new career. Your figure can decrease by the amount of income you'll receive after 59½, or even better, your 59½-year-old money can serve as a nice raise, a further hedge against inflation, or a safety in the case of unforeseen events. Or, you can go ahead and buy that boat, RV, or second home and fill it with beautiful things.

Decisions, such as where you'll live or how your lifestyle will change, don't have to be made now, but they are worth considering when evaluating different scenarios. If you own a home in an area with high housing values, you can probably count on large home equity growth. If you think you might leave the area after retirement and move to a lower cost one, your disposable income will stretch further. You might know where you want to live in your later years and consider buying a home and carrying it as a rental, with tax benefits, earlier rather than later.

You can get plenty of planning help from your bank, brokerage, or financial firm and through seminars sponsored by companies that want your business. Building a relationship with your bank is a good place to start. Get to know a personal banker and inform him or her of your long-term goals and earning potential. If you don't already have a broker, your bank relationship manager can introduce you to one within the bank. Banks have the computer software to help you with your income and expense estimates and inform you on the viability of your plan. You can learn how much you need to save and invest to meet your goal, and the analysis can show you when your dreams can become reality. There are also many investment sites on the Web that will help. One that comes highly recommended is *www.fundadvice.com/tools/calculators/index.html*. This site allows you to enter different scenarios, such as how long it would take to reach a savings goal, what rates of return you can expect from various investments, and the amount of money you will need to retire by a certain age. The resource segment of this chapter will show you more ways to measure "enough."

How much is ever enough? That answer completely depends on your value threshold. Clearly, the more you spend the more you'll need, and probably the longer you'll need to work at a high salary. If you have a good plan and a resource for ongoing advice, you will know the number you need to reach. If your freedom means everything you think it does, enough *will* be enough.

If your freedom means everything you think it does, enough will be enough.

7. LOOK GOOD, TAKE GREAT VACATIONS, AND DON'T FEEL DEPRIVED.

Saving and investing aggressively does not have to come at the expense of enjoying yourself in the present. From the time I started working, I bought myself a gift with every paycheck. Maybe it was just a new handbag or blouse in the beginning, but it was something. As my income grew, the quality of the gifts improved and though I kept the savings percentage of my gross the same (20 percent), I added a large part of my incentive payouts or bonuses. My disposable income grew as my income grew and I was always able to have nice things and great vacations, within my personal value threshold. I never felt deprived.

The secret is to live below your means and without debt, beyond your mortgage, if you can. I chose to keep my apartment and to fill it with things that I love rather than buy a bigger spot that would demand four times the monthly cash outlay. Keeping my monthly expenses low allowed me to save and invest for my freedom plan and have anything else I wanted in the meantime. Make a promise to yourself to pay your credit cards in full monthly. If you can't afford to pay something off, don't buy it. If something extraordinary comes up and you must charge it, do yourself a favor and try to find a credit card promotion that offers no interest for an extended period (e.g., six months). Work hard to pay the balance off within the allotted time to avoid heavy interest payouts at the end.

The secret is to live below your means and without debt, beyond your mortgage, if you can.

Having and keeping a low overhead will make your goal of financial freedom that much easier to reach.

8. DON'T WORRY ABOUT WHAT FRIENDS OR FAMILY MEMBERS SAY OR THINK ABOUT YOUR CHOICES.

Make your choices based on the life plan that you put into place for yourself and your family and don't worry about what other people say or think. For years, some of my friends would chide me about my one-bedroom apartment on the Upper West Side of Manhattan. I suppose it wasn't as luxurious as my job level would have called for, and I wasn't "keeping up" with my friends' lifestyles (or debt), at least in this way. I've always been very happy in my home and neighborhood and whenever I did look at real estate I could not see spending hundreds of thousands more to have a balcony the size of a table.

I have always worn nice clothes, but I won't spend $1,000 on a suit or $450 on a pair of strappy sandals that would go out of style the next season or break my ankle in this one. This spending did not suit my sensibility even though I could afford it and even though I enjoyed and admired their beauty. I willingly spend serious money on art, kitchen and tabletop, jewelry, furniture, or other items that I will enjoy for the long term. I take great vacations and dine out regularly. Another person might opt for the high-priced clothing versus a quick trip to the Caribbean, and another might decide they must have both. You make the choices and decide on the compromises that will get you to goal. These decisions did not feel like compromises to me, though. I was simply making a choice to always have choice. Your friends will stay your friends and they will revel in your happiness as you make changes in your life.

> *These decisions did not feel like compromises to me, though. I was simply making a choice to always have choice.*

9. BE AN ACTIVE INVESTOR. EDUCATE YOURSELF AND GIVE TIME TO YOUR FINANCIAL FREEDOM PLAN.

Make educating yourself about money a priority. Start simply with your bank relationship, reading the business section of your daily newspaper, and subscribing to a business or investment magazine or online newsletter. If you can attend investment seminars at no cost or low cost to you, do so. If you are new to investing, find a broker that you can feel stupid in front of, as I did. Be comfortable asking questions and if you are feeling intimidated, check your broker and yourself (you aren't expected to know everything at this early stage). If the broker is not willing to explain things in a way that you can understand, find someone else who will. Let the broker know of your income potential and build a relationship based on trust and growth for both of you.

At one point, early on, my portfolio took a dive because I was invested in bonds during the worst bond market since the Great Depression. As I read my statement, I panicked and flew out the door to my bank and other financial professionals for advice and opinion. All anyone could say was, "This is a disaster." It might not have been a lot of money in the grand scheme of things, but it was *all of my money*. I didn't change brokers then, but we did make a deal. I took responsibility for not being more involved with my money. It was *my* money, after all, and he was a broker, not a financial planner who worked on a fee basis.

I wanted my money back and the only way I could see to do it was to trade stocks like crazy for the foreseeable future. We negotiated a three-point plan: He gave me a very low commission rate on all trades for the next year, I committed to educate myself and become more involved, and we reserved one hour a week to discuss my portfolio, new financial news, and stock picks between the two of us. I closed my office door every Tuesday at 11 A.M. for a good many weeks. The need faded as I became more confident and as our strategy and trust grew more secure. I will never forget my first pick in our first week; it was for Pet Foods and I made $4,000 on the trade. In time I got my money back and my broker and I are still a solid team.

Develop a good relationship with your broker and meet in person a few times to see what your chemistry is. See if you can engage him or her to give you quality time on a regular basis to discuss your portfolio options, the economic climate, and companies that you have read about that you are interested in investing in. Close the office door and ask a lot of questions. Give yourself this gift. If your broker makes you feel uncomfortable about asking questions or

Be as assertive about your time regarding your financial future as you are about the most current issue at work.

seems impatient because you're not a big-money person at the moment, get a new one.

Consider that this is your money and your life, and you're working really hard for it. This is your future and it has to be important to the broker or planner and the banker you work with. You are paying this person to grow your money; it is that clear of a business proposition. Be as assertive about your time regarding your financial future as you are about the most current issue at work.

10. LOOK INTO RESOURCES.

If you want to learn about growing your wealth, the information is ubiquitous. A few books come to mind quickly. *You're 50, Now What: Investing for the Second Half of Your Life* by Charles Schwab contains valuable information about saving, investing, inflation, spending, and how to prepare for and enjoy a 40-year retirement. You will learn how much money you need to have invested for every 1,000 dollars you'll need per month and how much money you can take from your capital per year and still beat inflation. Don't wait until you're 50 to read this book; I wish I'd had it at 25. *The Millionaire Next Door* by Thomas J. Stanley, Ph.D. and William D. Danko, Ph.D., gives understandable ways to start your plan. Suze Orman's *The Road to Wealth* is a solid resource for someone seeking a fuller understanding of personal finance. New books come on the market constantly to answer all of your questions about personal finance and investments and don't be embarrassed to pick up an *Idiot's Guide to Finance*.

Magazines such as *Business Week, Fortune,* and *Money* are good sources for keeping up with trends and economic issues and profiles on companies and their leadership, in addition to expanding your knowledge about investing. Most financial magazines have an annual publication devoted to saving for retirement; read and save these special issues, or access them on the Web.

Online data is another way to keep informed. From CBSmarketwatch.com to sites from every business magazine and news channel, the information you want is as close as your fingertips. CNBC is a good channel to view from time to time to keep up on trends and for interviews with various CEOs and CFOs.

This chapter has been just the tip of the iceberg to get you thinking and started. You can grow your wealth, even in a bad economic time, if you take the responsibility to educate and align yourself with a team of professionals that includes at least a banker and a broker. Money is the foundation that your freedom plan depends on. Start as early as you can to become an active saver. Never be stuck anywhere because of money.

QUESTIONS

- What is your relationship with money?

- How important is freedom versus material goods to you?

- What do your spending habits say to you about your priorities? Are you comfortable with the message?

- Do you have a savings goal? Are you ready to commit to one?

- Do you have enough money to outlast a bad job market or a career switch?

- Do you have a basic understanding about personal finance? Are you ready to gain one?

- Will you clear an hour a week to converse with a broker about your investments?

- Will you create a personal relationship at your bank and have them run some numbers?

- Do you care what people think about your decisions? Too much?

- Can you limit the number of luxury items in your budget?

- Are you ready to make some tough choices about the way you handle your money?

- Might you consider beginning a financial freedom plan even if you are sure you want to work into your 70s?

25 WHEN LEAVING IS THE ONLY ANSWER

Ｈow will you know when it is time to leave your job or even change your career? You will know by the signals that your mind and body give you with regularity. You are unhappy and you don't see an upturn in the situation, although you have tried everything possible. Leaving your job is one thing, but leaving your career is a seismically more difficult achievement.

Switching jobs is a simple thing to do in good times. It's even doable in bad times if you've been mindful of your consistent delivery of excellent work, kept up with industry contacts, serviced your customers, and continued vitalizing training. Certainly the rule of getting a job while you still have a job might be heeded more than usual now because of the tough job market. In exceptional circumstances, such as the high number of job reductions in the technology sector, you might have to consider a career shift based on your skill sets or freelance in a related area to tide you over or start anew.

If you have decided to switch jobs, you've come to the conclusion that you need to go to a place where you can begin fresh, escape a toxic atmosphere, jump levels, increase your pay substantially, or a combination of these. In a much less exciting situation you might find yourself in a new job search because you've been laid off or even fired. The place you start a job search is the same, but the circumstance that brings you to it can alter your attitude about it. You might have to work hard to corral your self-talk so that you do not feel bad about yourself or too afraid about your future if the choice wasn't yours to begin with.

Hopefully, the same things you escaped at your last place won't appear in your next place. You're smarter as each year goes by in ways that matter beyond work. You know your values and your value, you know what it takes for you to be fulfilled in the workplace, and you are aware of what you offer a company for the long term. You are able to investigate people and places because you are an informed and valuable talent in search of a home that will be lucky to have you. You know the questions to ask and you are centered enough to make the right decision on your next place and next boss. You align yourself with a champion in the new place, reach great heights through stellar results, and retire with a fat 401(k).

You align yourself with a champion in the new place, reach great heights through stellar results, and retire with a fat 401(k).

Changing careers is a whole different matter. You might not even know what you want to do next because you haven't taken the time for reflection. You just need some quiet time to know yourself again, to involve yourself in activities, or learn something that has utterly nothing to do with your recent working past. Whether you know what you want to do next or not, leaving a career requires thought, patience, and a great deal of listening to yourself and the people you trust most.

If you are receptive to signals and change you will clearly know when the time is right. You will find that you have been working toward your life revision unconsciously for some time before the day of reckoning actually comes. For me, the manifestation was a hate reel in my head that I was unable to turn off. It culminated on the day that my finger refused to open my e-mail. It started a full year earlier when I moved my portfolio from 60 percent equities to 20 percent to preserve my capital. I remember being completely surprised to hear myself say aloud to my broker, "Paul, I think I'm getting ready to leave my career." It continued as I discussed a life change with my friends and family, and when my dearest friend told me I'd been very distant and low. It moved forward when a friend, my age, died suddenly, and it was made okay to me from an amazing dream that I had. It was made clear when I realized there was nothing else I wanted to do in the industry. I really had no choice but to go, because all bases were covered and all the answers were the same.

It took a year for me to gather the emotional courage and the feet-on-the-ground planning for a smooth transition. I considered and anticipated everything possible. I thought about interests and activities I hadn't had time for while I was working and used this information to prepare toolchests for my mental and emotional state in case I felt isolated or bored in my new life. I read books on finance, career change, and early retirement. I read spiritual books to make me feel better and I read memoirs to prove I wasn't crazy. I plotted a budget and checked it many times. Take your time and do what you need to prepare, as you stay as grounded as possible and do your best to deliver great work until your very last hour.

> *I really had no choice but to go, because all the bases were covered and all the answers were the same. Take your time and do what you need to prepare, as you stay grounded as possible and do your best to deliver great work until your very last hour.*

Some signs that your career end is near include these:

- Depression, especially when you are normally a positive and happy person.
- Anxiety attacks when none have occurred before.
- Stress headaches, or other physical ailments or changes such as a change in appetite.
- Dread every morning; interrupted sleep at night.
- You are pulling back from friends and family and isolating yourself more than normal.
- You are short-tempered at home and at the office, and your road rage is ridiculous.
- You don't really care anymore. You're going through the motions without personal investment.
- You are not interested in new initiatives or learning, when these were always your pleasure in the past.

- You start to think you hate the people that you work with, even when you know it isn't true.
- You feel bored and boring and not interested in anything new, in or out of your industry.
- You daydream a lot and see yourself doing something else. It could be just swimming, fishing, reading, cooking, laughing, or making love. You think and see yourself anywhere but where you are. You start to long for the parts of life missed.
- You look at the people who surround you with total disdain and watch their mouths move while you listen to nary a word.

You've reached the point where you must face the fact that this part of your life is over.

This is not an easy time and should not be taken lightly or handled alone. I relied on friends and family during this time but I could have gone further with them and probably benefited from some professional help as well. I was always so in charge of my life that to be this miserable was foreign to me and I was not eager to admit that the career I'd loved wasn't working for me any longer. I spent mornings in "heavy mental lifting," talking myself into being strong and the "old Joanne." Nobody at work knew the depths of my misery and I didn't discuss this so deeply with anyone else either. Instead, I worked harder than ever, worked on my exit plan, and probably isolated myself more than I should have or needed to. In retrospect, I believe this was a dangerous and needless way to handle this most challenging time in my life. A big life lesson for me through this time was that it is perfectly acceptable to ask people who love you for help and admit when something is really wrong.

> *You look at the people who surround you with total disdain and watch their mouths move while you listen to nary a word.*

Don't go down alone in business or in a tough time. Get the support you need; believe me, the people who you trust and who love you will want only what's best for you. People are willing to help you; all you need is the courage to ask them for it.

Rather than leaving abruptly, listen to the cues you receive and try to work to unparalyze yourself enough to start a plan B. Start with a personal support group, another board of directors to help you on your way out. Think about your passions, write lists, and prepare for the investigations you'll start once you leave. If you know what you want to do, start some diligence and preparation while you're still working. Create a business plan so you know what resources you'll need to get started. Plan a fall-off point in the form of a trip to a place you always wanted to visit but couldn't because you didn't have more than a week off at a time. Think of all the things you'd like to do and maybe, if you're prepared financially, give yourself four to six months to rest, heal, reflect and laugh out loud again; then you will be ready to move on.

Don't go down alone in business or in a tough time. Get the support you need; believe me, the people who you trust and who love you will want only what's best for you.

Leaving a career might be the toughest thing you ever do. It was for me. However, I can tell you I've never been happier. Opportunities for learning, living, loving, and experiencing things I've always hoped for have come into my life. I never would have had the time or openness to so many new adventures if I were still working like a maniac in a garage.

It's your life. Live it the way you want to.

QUESTIONS

- Do you find yourself in a situation that forces you to consider a career change?

- Have you been planning the career change that you've been thinking about?

- Is this turning into an obsessive reel in your mind?

- Are you noticing any physical changes that could be caused by this stress?

- Do you think you could use the help of a therapist, coach, or career counselor?

- Which family members or friends can you collect as a personal support group?

- Do you know what you'd like to do next? Do you realize that it is okay if you don't?

- Will you give yourself the time to start exploring forgotten passions?

- Can you start to plot a plan B and still be engaged in your work?

- Will knowing that you have started a plan B give you the peace and courage to go forward?

Summary of Part III: Planning for Passion and Prosperity

- Free agency must become an actual goal in today's tough job market. Become the "wow" hire in your industry. This does not condone job-hopping as a goal, rather it is creating your own security in a time when all calls are not necessarily yours to make. Follow the six steps outlined on page 188.

- The way you leave a company is important. Any move you make is about your future and not the past that brought you to it. The past is over and rehashing in anger won't change anything except what might be said about you in the future. Be as calm as possible, even if things get nasty. You might work with some of these people again, or jeopardize an exit package.

- Create your own Board of Directors by listing the pros and cons of a dilemma and matching the competencies required to solve the problem with people that can help you. Sometimes you have to go out of your immediate circle to include people that have had this experience in their own lives.

- Keep your passions and dreams alive until you are prepared to bring them to life. In the meantime, incorporate as much as you can into your daily work so that you can enjoy each day as much as possible.

- Gauge your level of fulfillment with the satisfaction checklist shown in Table 22-1 on page 202. By understanding what makes you happy or angst-ridden you will be more able to make changes in your life for better coping and more enjoyment and purpose.

- Bringing a spiritual aspect to your work doesn't mean becoming religious if you aren't. It means realizing your impact on the whole of the place and making the work more noble than the negative-speak in your head. When the work has a higher purpose for you it will transcend irrational behavior by disgruntled others and their impact on your head and heart will become less potent.

- A centered and balanced life must be a conscious goal today. Examine your life in terms of the mental, emotional, spiritual and physical aspects and see what you can do to become more balanced across them. Examine your mental and physical time spent at work, even if you aren't physically in the office, and see what you can do to bring it back to the middle. When you understand your motivations, you will have a clearer answer on how to create balance.

- Your personal identity drives action. Who are you besides this kingmaker extraordinaire? You are all of the people you love and interact with and you are all of the interests and passions that move you. Open your world and your own identity.

- Can you adopt the mantra "never be stuck anywhere because of money?" Will you take the time to understand your relationship with money and create a value threshold? Answer the questions on page 217 in earnest and see what you learn about yourself.

- Do you agree that excellence is your only work security and money is a main life security? You need money to make the calls in your own life, survive a bad job market or financial market, and make changes when you want to. Start as early as possible by becoming an invested, interested and serious money planner and manager. Give yourself the time and count it as a priority.

- You will know when it is the right time to switch jobs or shift careers. Listen to yourself and open up to the signs and opportunities that come your way. This is not an easy time and should not be taken lightly or alone. Seek help if you are sinking into depression. Realize that it is all right if you aren't sure what your next life goal will be. The answers will come as you prepare and anticipate and refresh.

- Work hard to deliver stellar work until your very last hour as you keep your eye on the biggest freedom and passion prizes of your life.

26 Your Personal Value Kingdom

We've covered a lot in this book that might have triggered some insight, or even a new outlook for you. Hopefully your commitment to excellence has been confirmed or reignited, your view has been enlarged beyond your normal thinking, and your empathy toward the people above, beside, and reporting to you has been engaged. Maybe you found a new way to look at an old situation and breathe new energy into it. Perhaps you've come to the realization that a new life change is in order for you, be it a job or role shift, a job or career change, or a freedom plan. Change isn't always easy, but change that you create for yourself beats change that is forced upon you.

Here's what we know:

- You're working harder than ever, yet you have to work smarter than ever to thrive and have a balanced life.
- You can give them what they want and still be you.
- Competent is average and you aren't average. Excellence is the only real security.
- You want to matter and you want your ideas to be heard without being perceived as resistant.
- You must search for the most effective way to communicate to your target so that he or she will best hear your message.

- You want to love what you do and be secure, respected, and promoted for what you do.
- You want your management to be smart and inclusive and you want your superiors to set a high bar and a good example.
- You want to be counted as a doer, a change agent, a mentor, and a champion.
- You want a champion in a high place to teach, trust, and advocate for you.
- You want to work within the rules, with the freedom to make them better.
- You want to be an employable free agent at all times, even if you love your current job and company.
- You want to be financially prepared for any eventuality so that you make the important calls in your life.

These orders aren't so tall that you can't handle them. The biggest challenge is to be flexible and willing while understanding yourself well enough to know your limits. Limits as used here doesn't mean shortcomings, it means finding the adaptability level that you are willing to meet to fit. The mantra to remember is that you are hired because of your special and unique talents and you decide who gets them. Part of your talent is your verve, insights, passion, and predisposition to success, however you define it. Adapting to fit is fine, but losing yourself and compromising your values on the way isn't. Flexibility is key, so keep your backbone strong because you'll need it to stay true to yourself and your dignity in difficult circumstances. Courage is yours to muster and it is within you. You display it each time you question the status quo, make a key presentation, create a new contact, or put yourself out beyond your last known comfort zone.

> *The mantra to remember is that you are hired because of your special and unique talents and you decide who gets them.*

At end of the day, or your career, you can look back, as I do, with real fondness for the time and the challenges. Even the stuff that you thought you couldn't get through will make you stronger, wiser, and better prepared for the next challenge in your life, inside or outside of your career.

Knowing that you jumped hurdles well only prepares you to confidently do it again. There is no room for regret in this scenario because you followed your heart and mind and chose the place you worked, the jobs you went for, and the promotions you won or didn't. You are better off because of all the things you tried and did, no matter the outcome on the measurable results chart. The you that you are in this world is your measurable result.

Your career is a great, long, uncharted voyage. There will be times of clarity and peaceful calm, and periods of roaring tempests and waves of turmoil. Your career is the sector of your life that will take up the most of your mental and emotional space and time, over time. Your world can change many times in the course of your life. People will come and go, friendships will ebb and flow, love will be lost and found, the economy will roar and plummet, the world will be at peace or at war, technology will surprise and move us, and through most of it all, we will be at work.

> *People will come and go, friendships will ebb and flow, love will be lost and found, the economy will roar and plummet, the world will be at peace or at war, technology will surprise and move us, and through most of it all, we will be at work.*

Your career cannot simply be the means to an end; it is just too big. Let it become a means to endless possibilities and passions and discovery in your life. Your career is a parallel life to the other parts of your world, and the larger world, which impacts us all. It is a pipeline that moves under the ocean, or a rail track that traverses mountains, hills, and plains. While all else is going on, your career exists, moves, thrives, and thrills you.

These pages are devoted to the honor and dignity of a great working life. A life in which generosity trumps greed, stretch is a given, curiosity is sated, willingness is necessary, and idealism can be wrapped in reality for great results. None of this can happen for you unless you make it happen for yourself, and one by one and together, the virtues will triumph over intermittent misery. Your attitudes, responsibility, sense of community, and desire for learning will keep you going. Your values will be consistent and refreshing for you as you respect your covenant and perpetually rejuvenate them.

The way you manage your career will make all of the difference in what it gives you and what you take from it. Your commitment to excellence, truth, anticipation, and planning will go a long way toward making the time you spend working meaningful and purposeful to your life and our world.

A life in which generosity trumps greed, stretch is a given, curiosity is sated, willingness is necessary, and idealism can be wrapped in reality for great results.

Career excellence is measured by results, your impact on others, your formal reviews, and the legacy you build. Life excellence is your own personal measure and might include the integrity you bring to any situation, the willingness to learn and grow, and your ability to tolerate and enjoy differences.

Career truth is manifested in your communication and in the trust that you build with those who surround you. Truth is alive in passion and new ideas, in the willingness to make a mistake, or in the courage to speak up when things aren't right. Truth is in holding onto your values and appreciating yourself and your contributions even if you are alone in this light sometimes.

Life truth is in being the same person inside and outside of the workplace.

Anticipation is a skill that will save you much fret. Think big to go past the mundane, the obsessions, constant change, political tyranny, and the competition in your career. If you are able to anticipate the actions or responses of others you will be prepared to handle and move beyond them. Think big in your career to increase your value, branding, and free agency, which will fortify your security and free you to do great work. Anticipate by first understanding. Anticipate your long-term goals and live openly to embrace new people, ideas and opportunities. Anticipate your monetary needs so that you will be ready for any eventuality.

There is simply nothing that eases your mind like preparation. When you know your stuff, nobody is better than you are, even if they don't agree with you. When you are prepared, you can handle any meeting, confrontation, boss, or change. Preparedness will give you confidence over ego, quash fear, and fuel your triumph over the competition. When you are prepared, you will enjoy your work, survive a job reduction, recognize new opportunity, and be more able to manage a balanced life.

Use the bad times you will encounter as a splash of cold water. Let it startle you into growth and understanding and, when necessary, change. Revel in the good times and do your most to create them and to make them long lasting and contagious. Find your truth, know yourself, understand the game, and give it all you've got.

QUESTION

- Are you ready to thrive on your terms?

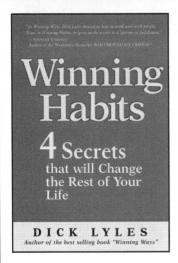